HEDGES & SCREENS

Roger Sweetinburgh

WARD LOCK LIMITED · LONDON

ACKNOWLEDGEMENTS

The publishers are grateful to the following agencies/photographers for granting permission to reproduce the colour photographs: Harry Smith Horticultural Photographic Collection (pp. 2, 15, 22, 27, 34, 42, 51, 83, 87 and 90); Photos Horticultural Picture Library (pp. 46, 55, 59 and 67); Pat Brindley (pp. 63 and 70); Peter McHoy (pp. 66 and 75); Andrew Lawson (pp. 42 and 58); and Edifice (cover and p. 31).

All the line drawings are by Roger Sweetinburgh.

Text © Ward Lock Limited 1989
Line drawings © Ward Lock Limited 1989
First published in Great Britain in 1989
by Ward Lock Limited, 8 Clifford Street,
London W1X 1RB, an Egmont Company.

House editor Denis Ingram

Text filmset in Bembo
by Hourds Typographica, Stafford

Printed and bound in Portugal
by Resopal

British Library Cataloguing in Publication Data

Sweetinburgh, Roger
　Hedges and screens.
　1. Gardens. Hedges.
　I. Title　II. Series
　635.9'76

　ISBN 0–7063–6756–1

HEDGES
& SCREENS

CONTENTS

PREFACE

Gardens mean different things to different people, but on the whole, most people prefer a degree of privacy and certainly some protection against prevailing winds. Obviously this can be achieved in a wide variety of ways, but it is often done without any real thought. With plant screens in particular, using the wrong plants can lead to a screen of overpowering density and proportions, instead of something light, attractive and only partial, as intended. This book will help you assess how much screening you need and to weigh up the various types of screen against each other. As well as information on all sorts of plants, there is helpful guidance on how to select and perhaps build timber, stone and other types of screen, with useful hints on taking care of them in subsequent years.

Perhaps, most of all, this book shows that far from being something which is simply tagged on to a garden, a screen is a vital part of an overall design and this should be taken into account right from the start.

R.S.

CHAPTER 1

DECIDING THE SIZE AND TYPE OF SCREEN NEEDED

There must be many reasons why a screen of some sort is needed in the garden. The more common reasons are to shut out overlooking windows, screen unpleasant sights like ugly walls or power lines, or to reduce the effect of prevailing winds. For those living by a road or railway, there could also be a need to reduce noise. In the latter instance very careful consideration should be given to choice of screening materials, for by no means all have the effect of reducing noise from road vehicles and trains. Noise from roads seems to be an increasing problem, with the development of new road systems and motorways.

There are so many ways of creating a screen that the right answer for a particular problem may use a combination of several ideas rather than just one. It is well worth considering all the possibilities before making any final decisions.

The first point to consider is exactly what degree of screening is needed. Perhaps it is only needed during the summer months. It may be needed for only a very small area and, even then, only up to a modest height. It may need to be instant and it may have to cost as little as possible.

A COMMON PITFALL

The usual reaction by someone anxious to screen their garden for a particular reason is to plant or erect the biggest and quickest barrier available at the time without too much thought for the possible consequences. A tall screen can work in either of two ways. If, for example, it was felt that a screen of tall evergreen trees or conifers placed along the boundary would be ideal to block out an upstairs window in a neighbouring building, the neighbours could well have a lot of light taken away from their property, if they happen to be on the shady side of the screen. But the opposite could happen, with the eyesore disappearing from view and *you* finding much of the sunshine gone along with it.

A MORE ACCURATE APPROACH

There are ways around this. The key is to work out exactly which areas need screening so that the size and position of the screen can be ascertained more precisely (Fig 1). It can be seen that the further away the screen is from the source of the problem, and the nearer to the person or spot that requires seclusion, the smaller it can be. Of course, the opposite is true. It is seldom that every corner of the garden needs screening — more often it is one or two especially sensitive areas, as where someone wants to sunbathe or dine in private. Perhaps it is one particular room in the house that needs extra privacy or, in the case of windy, exposed gardens, a screen might be needed where it will reduce the wind in one or two particular parts of the garden.

If a telegraph pole or distant pylon is the unwanted spectacle, several forms of screen could be employed at different points to take over from each other as one walks around the garden. In a more positive sense, a screen might be used to block out some views yet frame or accentuate others. For example, a gap could be left in a more general screen to allow a view through to a distant church spire, hill or other interesting object.

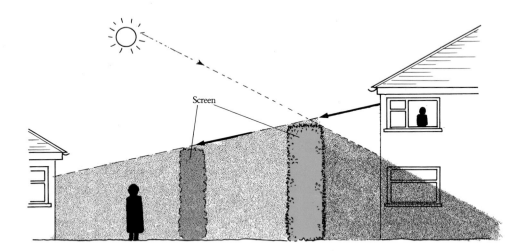

Fig. 1 A tall screen can provide a good deal of seclusion but often some unwelcome shade too. A smaller screen could be used if it was positioned closer to the area needing seclusion and less shade would result.

NARROWING DOWN THE POSSIBILITIES

A good way of assessing how tall a screen would need to be is to have one person standing, sitting or lying down in the 'sensitive' area while another moves away, holding up a pole so that the ideal height required can be assessed at various distances. It must be remembered that width is linked to height. The further away the screen is placed the higher *and* wider it will need to be.

Perhaps several smaller screens could be considered rather than just one large one. Despite working with a pole, it can still be very difficult to judge how effective a screen is going to be by just staring at an open space and trying to imagine it. A much more certain way of judging the likely effectiveness of small screens at least is to prop up a spare fence panel or two, support a sheet on some poles, or even pile up some garden furniture – anything to mock up the eventual screen.

TYPES OF SCREENS

Once the position and approximate size of a screen has been decided, the following points will need considering:
>   i) its density and thickness
> ii) whether it needs to be instant
> iii) formed of plants or a manufactured screen?
> iv) is it to screen visually or act as a windbreak?

Coupled with these general considerations, it is worth taking a broad look at each type of screen available before finally deciding what to use. Even if you come back to the first thing you thought of after all this effort, you can at least be confident that there was no better alternative.

EVERGREEN AND DECIDUOUS TREES, CONIFERS, SHRUBS AND HEDGES

It is vital to remember that plants never stop growing. Where trees and shrubs are being considered for an informal (rather than a clipped) screen, the screen is almost certainly going to begin smaller than required, go through a phase when it is acceptable and then perhaps end up by totally outgrowing its welcome. All plants have been 'programmed' to try and achieve certain proportions before they die and it is almost impossible to influence this significantly. If forest trees are chosen, then any pruning later in life will have to be on quite a large scale and be done skilfully if the trees are not to appear 'butchered'. Some conifers can be kept under control by constant clipping but unless some sort of scaffolding is used, you will only be able to reach to a limited height. The same applies to trees and large shrubs which are, hopefully, being kept in trim as hedges.

Another rather unfortunate feature of some conifers is that the bottom branches may die off, making screening at a lower level less effective. This is much more a problem with conifers that have been left to grow naturally and less likely to arise on regularly clipped plants.

As plants grow taller, most require additional width to develop properly. This can be kept in check by trimming or pruning but in a small garden their width might still take up quite a lot of space. With unclipped, natural screens, this width may be quite considerable. Added to this is a zone of soil, beyond the extent of the branches, which will be full of roots, relatively dry, and generally unsuitable for many other plants. Evergreen trees will obviously provide screening all the year round but do tend to look the same and may appear rather sombre. A greater variety of colour and interest is available from deciduous trees and shrubs. The merits and arrangements of different plants are discussed in more detail later in the book. If width has to be restricted to an absolute minimum it is worth considering climbing or wall-hugging plants growing against some sort of structure – this provides a compromise between having a largely plant-orientated screen without the excessive width.

WALLS, FENCES AND TRELLIS

Man-made screens offer a greater degree of control but also certain limitations. Although they can be built to a predetermined height and are therefore 'instant', there is usually a limit to that height.

More permanent structures like brick or stone walls are still not without significant width, since any foundation is supposed to be twice the width of the wall standing upon it. These structures are usually rather expensive but, on the other hand, permanent and maintenance free.

Fences are, in the main, slightly more limited in height but relatively inexpensive. Most are reasonably maintenance free and many are cheap enough to be replaced after a few years rather than maintained. Whether they are maintained or replaced can create problems if plants have become well established on or against them. The height of a fence can be increased with the use of trellis, but this can in turn make the whole structure more prone to wind damage. Really substantial fencing posts will help.

For more ornamental, lightweight screening, there are various kinds of trellis using both rustic and sawn timber. Their advantage over more solid structures is that they filter the wind rather than stop it altogether, which is often better for the garden and the screen.

They can also be constructed in a wide variety of styles and materials which, in itself, adds a good deal to a patio area or small garden. Some of the more elaborate architectural screens may be so ornate (and expensive) that it is positively wasteful to cover them in plants. Other structures widely available include concrete 'pierced screen blocks', columns and balustrading, bamboo and reed screens, screens made from glass and plastics and many combinations of these materials.

PLANTS VERSUS MANUFACTURED SCREENS

Plant material on its own gives the most natural effect, can achieve considerable height and density and can, to a certain extent, be controlled by regular clipping or pruning. On the other hand, plants can take a good deal of time to create a screen, take a lot of goodness out of nearby soil and demand much regular work if they are to be kept as a neat hedge.

Manufactured screens give instant results and screening to a predetermined height or density. They can range from very utilitarian and not particularly attractive through to highly ornamental. Unfortunately they are sometimes more expensive (initially) than a plant screen, not always long lasting and may need regular maintenance. The answer to a screening problem often lies in a combination of plants and a manufactured structure.

CHAPTER 2

DESIGNING THE GARDEN AND THE SCREEN TOGETHER

If no real effort has been made to work out the precise position and size for a screen, the most common answer, especially for small gardens, seems to be to plant or erect a screen all round the perimeter without giving much consideration to the rest of the garden layout. Even if the best place for it is around the outside, much can be done to ensure that a screen at least contributes to the beauty of a garden rather than spoils it.

SCREENING A PATIO

Take a patio as a specific example. It may well be that the best position for a patio just happens to coincide with the very spot which is over-looked by a neighbouring window at the further end of the garden. By carrying out some of the investigations described earlier, it will probably become apparent that some sort of screen close to the patio would provide the necessary seclusion. If the patio is very sunny and presumably quite hot at times, it might be worth considering an overhead pergola structure placed exactly in line with the offending view. (Fig 2) Because the viewpoint is quite high up on a neighbour's house, a low level screen might be less effective or at least need the addition of a pergola. When the offending window is immediately next door, the pergola idea could be even more effective, though its position would need adjusting. The density of the pergola is rather important. With too many cross members or too many large-leaved climbing plants, it might cast too much shade on the patio or in a room nearby. A screened patio is very much like a room – it has an atmosphere and can be effectively furnished with tubs, pots, climbing plants and, of course, garden furniture. Even if the area around the patio were a vast industrial wasteland, with skilful screening the patio could enjoy a world all of its own.

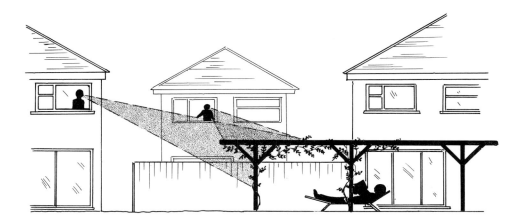

Fig. 2 A pergola can provide a certain degree of privacy, depending upon the density of climbing plants.

If the area next to the house is in permanent shade, then a patio further out into the garden might be more sensible. Once away from the house, a patio could be more vulnerable to being overlooked, but a wrap-around arrangement of screens or plants could help provide relative seclusion, so long as not too much shade is created.

SECLUDED SEATING

In gardens where an informal layout with partially hidden areas is wanted, plenty of opportunities arise for a secluded garden seat, tucked into a planted or screened corner. (Fig 3) There is a lot to be said for one seat positioned to catch the mid-morning sun with another elsewhere to catch the evening sun, in addition to the main patio. If screens seem rather unproductive, then some sort of summerhouse, or in larger gardens a gazebo, can give very localized seclusion. A gazebo is usually a small isolated patio often raised up above the ground with a pergola and maybe climbing plants over the top. Occasionally the open sides are partially screened with trellis, but usually the sides are left open to give a commanding yet secluded view over open countryside or across part of a large garden. A position which catches the evening sunshine is often favoured, providing a pleasant destination for an evening stroll around the garden or estate.

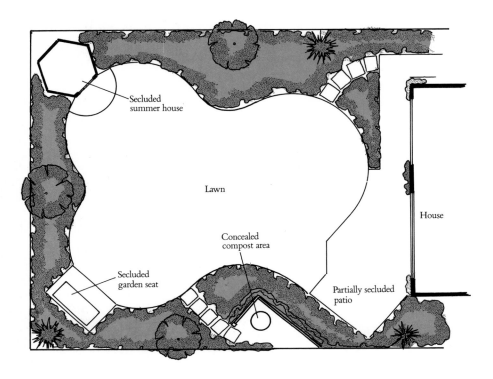

Fig. 3 A garden with several partially secluded areas.

SCREENING DISTANT VIEWS

Screens can be used in many selective ways. There may be a rather unsightly outlook beyond the garden except for, perhaps, one small point of interest in the distance. If screening is arranged to cut out all the unpleasant views but leave the open point of interest, it can actually emphasize the attractive feature and allow the eye to travel beyond the confines of the garden. The screen need not be of trees or shrubs but perhaps a long trellis with one or two arches to accentuate and frame the better views.

Opposite: A complete screen around the patio can create the feeling of an outdoor room. Climbing plants would soften the overall effect.

COMPOST HEAPS AND BIN STORES

On a more localized scale, compost heaps and bin stores may need screening while leaving access unimpeded. Overlapping screens or screens built in a circular fashion can be very useful here. Anything more localized than this becomes an attractive cladding on the compost box or shed itself.

In more general terms, some consideration should be given to style. A cottage will often look better with a rustic trellis screen than a modern concrete block wall. A sawn timber trellis using quite heavy timbers would probably suit a modern house in woodland surroundings while an older, brick residence would indicate the need for brick walls, and so on. Plants tend to be compatible with all these situations.

GROUND MODELLING

Ground modelling or mounding, especially in large gardens or estates, can reduce noise from a road or railway and will help to create some seclusion but only, usually, at a fairly low level. Unfortunately, some ground modelling can funnel the wind and create problems in that way.

Ground modelling obviously affects the rest of the garden layout, making it almost imperative for this type of screening to be included in the overall design. Major ground modelling needs a lot of careful preparation and is skilled work best tackled by an expert. However, it is as well to remember that the mounds will have to be topsoiled afterwards since they will probably be formed largely of subsoil which is unlikely to grow plants (including grass) very well. If the topsoil is to come from within the plot, it will have to be stripped and stored somewhere while the rest of the earthmoving is taking place. This requires a lot of space and can be very disruptive in an already mature garden.

SCREENS

PANEL FENCES
Timber screens can best be divided up according to their density. Those which are virtually impossible to see through are usually classed as fences or dense screens and are often available as manufactured panels. (Fig 4) Two of the most common versions are horizontally lapped and interwoven 'larch' panels, though larch is not the only timber used. The lapped version is designed to remain 'peep proof' even when the timber

Fig. 4 Two common types of panel fence. (*a*) Interwoven fence; (*b*) Larch lap fence.

slats have shrunk with age, whereas the interwoven types do become less peep proof with age and may be less expensive to buy. These and other types of panel are often around 1.8 m (6 ft) long but can be bought in various heights – perhaps as high as 2.4 m (8 ft).

Another very common type of fence is 'close board' which is available as panels or in kit form. This type of fence has vertical, overlapping slats or 'pales' of timber which are thinner down one edge than the other – feather edged. The kit form of this fence is more common than the ready-made panels. Generally speaking, all panel fences have to be stepped down a hillside because of their squareness but the kit form of the close board fence does enable it to follow a slope in a smooth line.

RUSTIC HURDLES
A number of more rustic or informal types of fencing are available in panels. These are referred to as woven 'wattle hurdles' and are made from horizontally woven branches of hazel (*Corylus*) or willow (*Salix*) and occasionally other materials too. The willow hurdles are more dense and more precise than their hazel counterparts but both can be quite long-lived in sheltered positions.

REED AND BAMBOO
Screens of vertically woven reeds or bamboo can give an oriental flavour to the garden. Some reed panels are very thick and can last very well but the thinner, split bamboo screens, which may come in a roll rather than as a rigid panel, do not last so well, particularly in wetter climates.

The rolls of split bamboo obviously have no frame of their own and have to be attached to one. This could be an old fence whose framework is still sound. Alternatively, a bamboo screen can be fixed on to tight wires across the face of an ugly wall – being used almost like wallpaper. Its uses are numerous but its doubtful ability to remain looking good in wet conditions limits its use to shorter term projects.

SAWN TIMBER TRELLIS

Less dense than fences and hurdles are the various trellises. The simplest of these is probably the square type where a series of timbers cross over at 90° producing square or diamond-shaped spaces. These timbers are usually 'laid on' and nailed. The timber can either be rough sawn or planed smooth. Much more elaborate and attractive trellis can be made from thicker planed timber which is lap jointed to give a flush finish (Fig 5). This type of trellis is very architectural and is especially effective around patios or when used to break up expanses of boring wall. While rough sawn trellis is usually stained brown or perhaps green, the planed timber types can be much more easily painted or given a coloured stain (including white). The uprights for these more elaborate panels need not be square in section – hexagonal posts are sometimes used with ornate tops which can be repeated at intervals along the tops of the panels themselves. Any pattern can be employed in trellis work, even circles, but the joinery may then become very involved and intricate.

TIMBER TREATMENT AND PRESERVATION

All the timber structures mentioned so far (with the possible exception of the hurdles and bamboo screens) can have their life dramatically

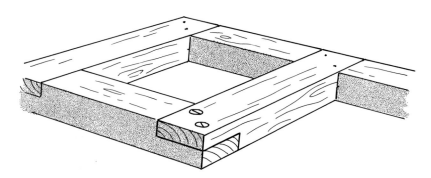

Fig. 5 Half-lap joints can be fixed with rustproof screws or with pins and water-proof adhesive. The timber must have been treated against decay.

extended by treatment with various types of preservative. With so many products now available, it is relatively easy to select something suitable for most situations.

The most thorough treatment is a technique which impregnates timber with a preservative under pressure. This process has to be carried out in a special tank so the timber is sold already treated. The most susceptible part of any fence or trellis is its posts or uprights. Rotting can quickly take a hold at the point where the post enters the ground. This is where bacteria and fungi work quickest in the presence of air and moisture, so that posts at least should be treated in some way.

It may be more difficult to buy fence panels which have been pressure treated, so some other type of treatment, either sprayed or brushed on, would be more usual here. Creosote has been used for many years, combining preservative qualities with staining, but it does smell strongly and can burn nearby plants. More recent products tend not to smell so strongly nor burn plants so readily. It is much more usual now to consider preserving timber as a separate process from colouring. This has been partly brought about by the fact that ready pressure treated timber needs no further preservative but may need colouring. Most modern methods of colouring timber involve the use of products which allow the timber to breathe. This means that the product is unlikely to peel or flake and re-decoration is as easy as washing the surface clean and just applying an extra coat. Whichever product is used, plants will have to be moved out of the way and replaced only when the product has dried.

RUSTIC TRELLIS
As the density of the screen diminishes, its role changes from being a screen in its own right to becoming a framework over which plants can be trained. This is true of rustic trellis which tends to employ rather straight poles sparsely arranged in a largely horizontal, vertical or diagonal pattern. In Victorian times the timber would have been more gnarled and bent, making the rustic trellis more of a feature in its own right.

The poles are either stripped of their bark (and often pressure treated) or have their bark left on. Some timber is not pressure treated because it is resilient against rotting. Most hardwoods come into this category, including sweet chestnut (*Castanea*) and oak (*Quercus*). Branches of silver birch (*Betula*) rot far too quickly to be of any use.

In days gone by when pressure treatment was not available, poles were made resistant to rotting by having the bottom portion charred in a fire. Another possibility is to put preservative in a deep drum and stand the bottom portion of the pole in it for for 24 hours. It must be remembered that all these treatments need to cover the part of the pole which is at or close to the ground surface. Treatment of the horizontal (structural) poles is less important. The effective height of a rustic trellis is usually higher than the structure itself because the climbing plants will extend above the top bar. This implies that the trellis need not be quite so high as at first thought. The opposite is true of arches, however, which need to be at least 2.1 m (7 ft) high to avoid any hanging branches or fronds from catching in people's hair as they walk underneath.

HEAVY ARCHES AND PERGOLAS

Once a heavier structure is needed, to keep in proportion with its surroundings or to support heavier plants, poles will have to be abandoned for wooden beams or even brick or stone supports. An arch constructed like this will obviously look much more substantial than a rustic one, especially during the winter when most of the climbing plants will lose their leaves. When this type of construction is extended to cover a paved area or a whole walkway, it becomes a pergola, in effect, giving the area it covers a degree of seclusion. The thickness of the cross supports and uprights must be in proportion to the surroundings. Large stone pillars with very thick cross beams might look rather silly in a very small suburban garden, but conversely thin timber uprights and cross beams would look equally unsuitable in a very large garden. Many pergolas rely purely on a series of uprights and cross beams without diagonal supports or bracing. This can make the whole structure rather unstable once plants have developed, especially in windy or snowy weather. To minimize this, the uprights must be very securely fixed in the ground and should not be too flimsy.

VERTICAL SCREENS

A very simple form of screen can be created by setting thick poles, wooden beams or even railway sleepers vertically in the ground. (Fig 6) They would obviously need a good portion in the ground for stability and a generous amount above it for screening. Their density can be varied by the distance they are set apart and can be increased with the addition of climbing plants. These may need some inconspicuous netting to help them establish up the face of the screen. One extra bonus of this type of screen is that it can be made to curve – quite steeply if necessary. This is a useful and pleasing feature for internal screens, if not for boundary screens which normally have to be straight. Curving screens are far more pleasing aesthetically yet surprisingly are all too rarely seen in gardens. The majority of people have yet to be "cured" of thinking only in terms of straight lines!

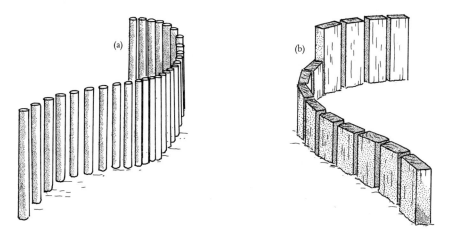

Fig. 6 (*a*) Treated, rustic poles can produce a screen up to 2.4 m (8 ft) high. (*b*) Railway sleepers produce a lower, sturdier screen.

METAL ARBOURS

One idea which has been used a great deal in the past to give some seclusion is the arbour. While this can take many forms, the quickest type to establish consists of a metal dome or framework over which vigorous climbing plants can grow. Beneath the metal work is an area of paving accommodating a garden seat. Metals which will not rust nor need maintaining are essential and the arbour should be positioned where it gives welcome shade in a spot with a good view of the garden or surrounding countryside. In many respects it is like a ground-level gazebo, relying more heavily on vegetation. There are many other forms of arbour, some using trees rather than climbing plants, but all have the same purpose of creating a shady nook for sitting in.

BRICK WALLS

Brick, stone and concrete are the obvious materials to consider if a more substantial, permanent and perhaps larger screen is needed. In some districts planning permission may be needed for a wall over about 1.5 m (5 ft) high, especially if it borders a public footpath or roadway. It is always worth checking with the local authority before starting work.

   The construction of high brick walls is probably best left to an expert

A remote patio can often be created in an already secluded corner of the garden: a perfect shady retreat on a hot summer's day.

but there are a few general points worth noting:

Brick walls are usually either 115mm (4½in) or 225mm (9in) thick. The thinner walls will need piers at intervals but very tall walls (the kind that might surround a walled garden) will need to be the full thickness and have piers or buttresses. When a pier occurs at the end of a wall, perhaps to hold a heavy gate, it will have to be a generous thickness and perhaps have steel reinforcing running up through the centre. House walls differ from garden walls in the amount of their exposure to the weather. They are well protected, being exposed on only one face, whereas garden walls are exposed all round.

THE TYPES OF BRICKS TO USE

To resist constant rain, frost and snow, garden walls should use 'stock' quality (or possibly 'engineering' quality) bricks. The 'flettons' which are often used in house construction are simply not hard enough to withstand the weather and often break up in heavy frost. The stock brick is more expensive than the fletton and so it may be cheaper and more appropriate to have a wall with brick piers, a brick top and bottom but large panels of concrete blocks between. These may not look attractive and so may need 'rendering'.

RENDERING FOR LESS ATTRACTIVE WALLS

In this process a mix of cement and sharp sand is applied with a plasterer's trowel or float as a thin layer over the surface of the blocks. When it has dried, it can be decorated with special paint or perhaps given a Tyrolean finish. This is achieved by splattering a sand and cement mixture on to the wall with a special machine. This is quite a skilled job though not totally beyond the ability of a keen amateur. One drawback of a Tyrolean finish is that it does tend to collect dirt on its eneven surface and may need repainting more often than a smooth, rendered surface.

DAMP PROOFING

A problem with all rendered surfaces is rising damp. If the wall is not protected against dampness in some way, the rendering might eventually begin to come off. This can be overcome by incorporating a damp course within the wall and by treating the back of the wall with a waterproofing compound. The type of membrane (plastic or bitumastic) normally used in house walls is not totally satisfactory when used in a free-standing garden wall because it creates a point of weakness. If pushed hard enough, the wall would break at the point of the damp course. In recent years, one or two rows of engineering bricks have been used just above ground level. These have the advantage of stopping rising damp yet at the same time preserve the wall's strength. A further damp course on or close to the top of the wall will help to stop rain working its way too far down. This can be backed up by fitting coping to the top of the wall. Waterproofing products which can be used on vertical surfaces like the back of the wall include bitumastic compounds, resins and silicones. It is unwise to grow plants which attach themselves with suckers to walls that have been rendered, this creates problems when it comes to re-decorating.

RECONSTITUTED STONE WALLS

Re-constituted stone blocks can be used instead of concrete blocks and are sometimes cheaper than bricks. Being made of concrete with a high proportion of natural stone, these have an attractive appearance and do not need rendering. They are, however, still very precise and artificial and are no real substitute for the real thing. These blocks are often available in different sizes so that a more random pattern can be created, and the use of different rock during their manufacture gives a choice of colour. There is no doubt this type of walling is very popular today, especially with owners of modern gardens. The blocks are readily available from local garden centres and from several well-known DIY stores.

NATURAL STONE WALLS

Walls made from pieces of natural stone tend to be thicker than the previous type of wall. Many different types of stone can be used and all but the very softest are suitable. Those which occur naturally as squarish, block-shaped or flat pieces are the easiest to use but some cutting and chipping is necessary, to get various pieces to fit together neatly. This can be very time (and stone) consuming, especially in the hands of a total novice. As it is difficult enough to achieve one smooth side (fair face) to a stone wall, it is common practice to erect a concrete block wall as a backing. Metal ties have to be incorporated as work progresses to hold the two together and the small gaps which inevitably occur between the back of the stone and the concrete blocks are packed with mortar to create a solid wall perhaps 450mm (18in) thick, depending on the type of stone. These walls can be made especially attractive by including a window here and there – possibly round, and positioned in such a way as to frame a particular view. Wrought iron work could be added to match a nearby wrought iron gate.

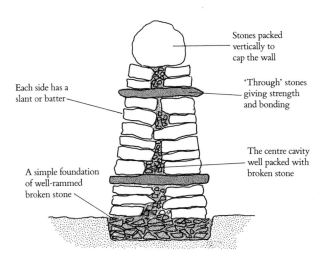

Stones packed vertically to cap the wall

Each side has a slant or batter

'Through' stones giving strength and bonding

A simple foundation of well-rammed broken stone

The centre cavity well packed with broken stone

Fig. 7 A free-standing dry stone wall.

FREE-STANDING STONE WALLS

All the walls so far mentioned have used mortar as part of their construction. But 'dry' stone walls have no mortar and rely for their strength on a good, interlocking fit between the stones. Construction of these walls requires a high degree of skill, especially if they are to be produced to any appreciable height (Fig 7). Even so, it is rather unusual to find them higher than, say, 1.5 m (5 ft) and because they are free standing, they have to be quite thick at the base and taper (batter) towards the top.

All walls can be produced in a curve. The tightness of the curve will depend to some extent on the size of the unit used. Bricks will permit a very tight curve but concrete and reconstituted stone blocks, which are obviously larger than bricks, have to be kept to a more gentle curve, otherwise the joints will open up too far on the 'back' side.

CONCRETE PIERCED SCREEN BLOCKS

Using larger blocks than most of the previous walls, concrete screen block walls are less adaptable when it comes to curves. However, a moderate curve can be achieved, provided the back or convex surface is kept out of view. The blocks are produced as a pattern created by holes or spaces right the way through. When mortared together, they create an overall pattern which can be quite pleasing in the right surroundings.

They obviously form only a partial screen and do not give complete privacy. Their density can be increased with plants but these in turn tend to mask the attractiveness of the wall. The blocks are stacked on top of one another and not bonded as bricks might be in a wall, so the wall is not particularly strong. To help, regular piers have to be incorporated. These can be constructed from matching 'pilaster' blocks or, more attractively, from brick or natural stone with a matching foundation wall.

There are also some terracotta products, rather like roof ridge tiles which, when fitted together give an attractive perforated and highly profiled wall. The overall effect is quite different to that created by the concrete blocks. The terracotta wall looks more at home with brick walls and paving than with concrete products.

BALUSTRADES

Screening at a lower level can be achieved by using balustrading. This is usually available in kits with horizontal mouldings for the base and coping, and vertical columns in different styles. Most are produced in reconstituted stone but some are produced or carved from natural stone and these are obviously quite expensive. Balustrading is seldom higher than about 1 m (3 ft 3 in) but its very presence along the edge of a terrace can provide anyone sitting behind it with some feeling of privacy.

OTHER FENCES

Most other fences, not so far mentioned, including those made from wire, and others constructed as post and rail fences, do not offer much in the way of privacy but usually protect gardens from straying people and animals. However, many of these fences can support growing plants and become effective screens. More detail is given on this later in the book.

GLASS AND PLASTIC SCREENS

Gardens near the sea or on windy hillsides may command beautiful views while being too exposed for anyone to enjoy them. So some form of screening seems essential.

There are many examples of screens constructed mainly from glass or

If enough space is available, wide borders around the lawn can eventually produce a completely secluded oasis.

plastic. Both these materials are vulnerable to damage and being solid, are specially vulnerable to wind damage. Any framework holding glass or plastic will have to be exceptionally strong.

Glass must be toughened or armoured – not just against the wind but also against vandalism. Wired glass has the advantage of not scattering its pieces far and wide but does have a visible matrix of wires. Toughened glass may seem alarmingly flexible but is very strong and resilient. The best plastics are acrylic and polycarbonate. Acrylic is very transparent but scratches easily. Polycarbonate may, in fact, be opaque so is less suitable for a view but excellent for diffused light. Plants silhouetted against an opaque screen can produce some very interesting effects. All these materials seem to be damaged more easily when they are cold.

CHAPTER 3

CONSTRUCTION OF SCREENS, WALLS AND FENCES

CONCRETE FOUNDATIONS

All walls which are held together with mortar should, ideally, have a rigid foundation thick enough to remain stable and to keep the wall from cracking or falling over. An exception is the freestanding dry stone wall which can flex with natural ground movement without fear of cracking or, hopefully, of falling over. It does, however, require reasonably firm ground perhaps with well rammed rubble foundations.

THICKNESS
Most wall foundations are constructed of concrete. Their thickness will depend upon the weight of the wall and the softness of the ground. Ideally, the foundation should reach down into firm ground, although in some situations this implies a very deep foundation indeed. This can be overcome by sinking piles but that, together with the construction of high walls, is beyond the scope of this book except for screen block walls. It is not easy to generalize for foundations but, as a rough guide, those in clay will need to be quite thick to stand up to the flexing that takes place when clay expands and contracts. A wall 225 mm (9 in) thick and 1.2 m (4 ft) high might need a foundation 225 mm (9 in) thick in clay (or very soft soil) but perhaps only 100 mm (4 in) thick in hard, stony soil.

POSITION
If a wall is to form a boundary between two properties, then the position of its foundation can be critical. Very often, in order to get the back face of the wall precisely on the boundary, it is necessary for part of the foundation to be in a neighbouring garden. The legal implications of this need careful investigation. If paving is to be laid up to the wall, the surface of the foundation will have to be far enough below ground to permit both the slab and its mortar to be positioned over the top. As a general rule,

the foundation must be twice the width of the wall upon it and always be laid dead level in both directions.

DIGGING AND PREPARING THE FOUNDATION

A string line will be needed to ensure that the foundation is exactly where it should be. A trench is dug to an appropriate depth, hopefully into firm soil. If the soil seems soft to a considerable depth and it seems pointless having the foundation floating on top of soft soil, there are two possible courses of action (other than pile foundations). One is to dig down until the soil begins to firm and then build back up to a reasonable depth with well rammed hardcore. The other is to put the concrete foundation in at a very deep level, then construct the bottom part of the wall with concrete blocks to just below ground level before changing over to a more attractive material. Whatever method is used, thin wooden pegs are inserted at regular intervals down the centre of the trench so that their tops indicate where the surface of the eventual concrete will be. These peg tops must all be dead level with each other.

THE CONCRETE

The concrete will comprise cement, 'all in ballast' and water. The cement and ballast are measured by volume – shovels full or buckets. An average mix, adequate for most occasions, would be one part of cement to six of ballast. Water is added and thoroughly mixed in until a stiff mix is achieved. The concrete is then placed in the trench. (Pouring indicates too wet a mix). It is spread between the pegs and rammed (tamped) into position with a block of wood until it is flush with the peg tops. If the pegs are thin, they can be left in.

Because concrete needs time to cure and must not dry out while this is going on, it should be covered with a sheet of polythene for a day or two. In cold weather, curing will take longer – perhaps as long as a week and frost or freezing will destroy or significantly weaken the concrete. These conditions should therefore be avoided, even if a frost-proofing liquid can be mixed in.

STEPPED FOUNDATIONS

On sloping ground, the concrete will have to be stepped up or down to keep pace with the ground. This can be known as a stepped foundation. Arrange the stepping to ensure that the concrete will never be visible above ground. If the concrete is quite a long way below ground and cheaper materials are used to bring the wall up to ground level, these materials must be capable of withstanding constant dampness. Very often the soil which comes out of the trenches can be re-used. Make every

A woven wattle hazel hurdle gives a country feel to any garden, especially when climbing plants are added.

effort to keep the topsoil separate from the subsoil, as the latter is unsuitable for plant growth. Work is easier if the soil is stacked on one side of the trench only, so there is clear access for wheelbarrows of concrete.

SCREEN BLOCK WALLS

Screen block walls are not the easiest type of wall to erect but the units are quite large, so the wall grows reasonably quickly and looks very attractive when finished. Most of the 'blocks' measure about 300 mm (12 in) square. To go with these are pilaster blocks which are built up into piers. Copings and caps are available to go on top of the finished wall and piers. Since pilaster blocks are about 200 mm (8 in) square, this indicates a foundation 400 mm (16 in) wide even though the screen blocks themselves are only about 100 mm (4 in) thick. Natural stone or brick piers can be used instead of pilaster blocks and can significantly improve the look of the wall but they require a higher degree of skill to construct.

TOOLS

The following tools and equipment will be needed to construct the wall (Fig 8):

    A string line and 'pins' to anchor each end
    A spirit level, bricklayer's trowel and pointing trowel
    Shovel, sand, cement, water and a mixing board.

The spirit level must have a vertical bubble as well as one for the horizontal plane.

The mortar mix, measured in volume, is made up from one part of cement to about six parts of soft sand, together with a plasticiser and, of course, water. The plasticiser will make the mix smoother, stickier and easier to work with. Ideally, the mortar should be quite moist and soft.

BUILDING THE WALL

A set of pilaster blocks will be needed every 2–2.5 m (6 ft 6 in–8 ft 4 in) including, of course, a set each end to finish off the wall. Screen blocks tend to be very porous, so if they are dry when laid they take a lot of moisture out of the mortar. This in turn produces weak joints and poor adhesion. The blocks should therefore be given a good soaking an hour or so before they are used. It helps if screen blocks and pilaster blocks are set out in line beside the foundation so they are to hand when needed. Place mortar on the foundation in a broad sausage shape with the builder's trowel, then press a groove down the middle, spreading the mortar outwards until it is almost the full width of the screen blocks – a

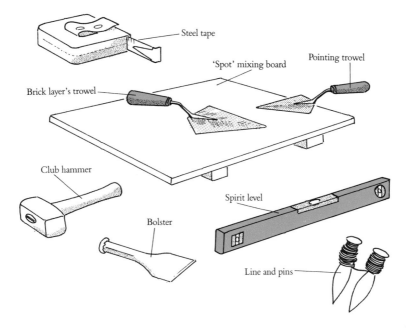

Fig. 8 Some useful tools for wall construction.

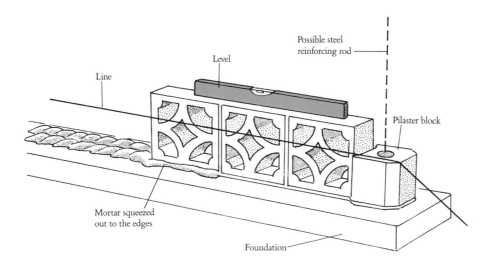

Fig. 9 Building a screen block wall.

An interesting effect is produced when an informal woven wattle (willow) hurdle is framed with painted, prepared timber.

little wider where the pilaster blocks are to go. A string line will be needed, supported at each end, to control the line of the wall. The end pilaster blocks can be left out of the structure to begin with so that laying starts with a screen block. Set this gently but firmly on to the mortared foundation, making sure it is level and vertical and that the mortar has been squeezed out to the edges (Fig 9).

A mortar joint should end up about 10 mm ($\frac{3}{8}$ in) thick. The next screen block will need a sausage of mortar on the side which is to be placed up against the first block. This can best be done by having that side uppermost and placing the mortar upon it just as it was placed on the concrete foundation. If the block or the mortar is too dry, the mortar will fall off as soon as the block is turned on its side. Assuming this does not happen, the block is pushed firmly down and in towards the first block until it is fixed firmly to it and is well bedded on to the foundation. It may be necessary to prevent the first block being disturbed by steadying it with one hand. The level and plumbness of this second block will need checking as quickly as possible to ensure it is in line, level and vertical. If the blocks are disturbed, even quite soon after laying, the suction and bond between them will break.

This process is continued all along the first row, inserting pilaster blocks where necessary. The pilaster blocks are shorter than the screen blocks but will coincide with the tops of every second row of screen blocks.

THE SECOND ROW

The second row is trickier than the first because the face of the wall begins to grow and has to be kept flush and vertical. As the number of joints increase, 'pointing' will have to be done, usually with a smaller 'pointing' trowel. The excess mortar is first scraped off the side of the blocks and then given a 'finish' by pressing and sliding the point of the trowel along the join (Fig 10). This is an important operation since it gives the wall its final appearance. Any mortar which has made spill marks down the face of the blocks will need to be wiped away with a damp or wet rag. To help strengthen the wall, flat pieces of expanded metal can be placed horizontally across the joints between the blocks as 'ties'.

As the wall grows, the end pilaster blocks should be added and incorporated, building them up at a similar rate to those in the rest of the wall. If the wall progresses quickly, it might be wise to leave it for a few hours before proceeding further so that the blocks already laid can partially set.

Finally, caps and copings can be added as a finish, making sure they strike a smooth and perfectly horizontal line. It is important to remember that the spirit level should be kept in constant use throughout construction. A string line should always be in position across the top of the blocks to keep the wall straight. A more professional technique is to set the string dead level by temporarily building up blocks at the far ends and laying the intermediate blocks so that their tops line up exactly with the tight, level line. The work must still be constantly checked with the spirit level. If the blocks are very light in colour, or even white, the mortar can be made as light by using whitish sand and white cement.

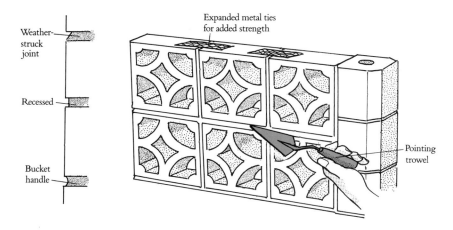

Fig. 10 Pointing up the mortar in a screen block wall.

ERECTING A PANEL FENCE

The easiest situation in which to erect a panel fence is level ground, with low panels and little or no wind. So describing how to erect tall panels on sloping ground on a breezy day should cover all the likely problems.

THE MATERIALS
Most fence panels are about 1.8 m (6 ft) long, with a variety of heights up to about 2.1 m (7 ft). Posts are generally of timber or concrete. The concrete ones are available with grooves down opposite sides to accommodate the fence panels. Timber posts are usually treated with preservative. Posts should go at least 375 mm (15 in) into the ground. They usually protrude as much as 50 mm (2 in) above the panels, once fixed, which

suggests that the posts for a 1.8 m (6 ft) high panel need to be at least 2.25 m (7 ft 6 in) long and preferably 2.4 m (8 ft). On sloping ground, posts may need to be longer. (Fig 11). Gravel boards may be necessary at the bottom of each panel, especially on sloping ground, to fill out the difference in soil level. Gravel boards are timber or concrete panels about 200 mm (8 in) deep fixed horizontally on or in the ground at the foot of each panel. In practice, the fence panel may rest on the gravel board. Galvanized nails will be needed, a claw hammer, string line, spirit level and various tools to dig out holes and ram in soil or hardcore (broken bricks, etc). Materials for making concrete will be needed if concrete posts or metal sockets are being used. Metal sockets are available into which the wooded posts can be slotted, and these sockets are normally concreted into position. Metal brackets are also available. These are fixed to the posts and the panels are slotted into them in much the same way as they might be slotted into grooved concrete posts (Fig 12).

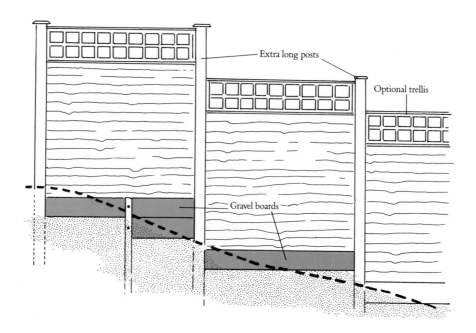

Fig. 11 Panel fencing on sloping ground.

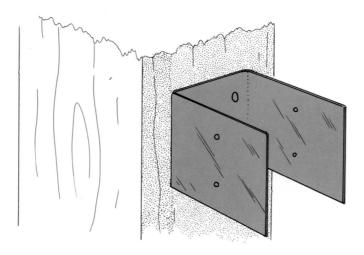

Fig. 12 A galvanized steel bracket to hold panel fencing.

THE LINE OF THE FENCE

The line of any fence can be critical if it is to form part of a boundary. If difficulties are likely to arise over its positioning, legal advice should be taken. It seems to be usual to have all the structural cross members of a fence facing the owner and the smoother, more attractive side facing outwards. This is one way of deciding who a fence belongs to, though it is not foolproof.

POSITIONING THE POSTS

Once a string line is down it is well worth measuring along it to ascertain exactly where the posts are to go. If the new fence replaces an old one, the remains of the old posts and even large pieces of concrete could well coincide with the new posts. If this is so, there are two options. Either remove these obstructions (often very hard work) or start with a half panel so that the new posts miss the obstructions.

FIXING POSTS

The holes can be dug by hand, using a normal or extra narrow spade, or hand auger (like a huge corkscrew) or, on a larger scale, powered auger. A powered auger will either have its own motor and be hand held (perhaps by two people), or tractor mounted.

This screen could act as a localized windbreak as well as provide some privacy. Plants could be introduced to soften the overall effect.

Concrete posts and metal sockets can be concreted in using a stiff 'one in six' mix but this technique is not recommended for timber posts. Timber posts tend to rot at ground level, especially if they are set in concrete so they are best held with well rammed hardcore which will help to keep soil away from the timber and water drained away. Before posts are put in the ground they must be marked so that the right amount goes below ground level, leaving sufficient above ground to support a panel and protrude just a little above it. A spirit level is essential to get the post exactly vertical. If the post is being concreted in, it will have to be left to set before continuing. This places a severe restriction on progress, so, if possible, it is worth concreting a whole series of posts into position, provided this is done perfectly accurately. Two string lines will be helpful, one aligning the bottom of the posts, the other keeping the tops in line. On sloping ground, it is very difficult to estimate exactly how much each post should be above ground, since the panels will step up or down each time. In these circumstances, it is best to erect the fence as you go, using an especially stiff concrete mix to hold the posts firm.

OFFERING UP THE PANELS

Once the first post is in, a panel can be placed gently up to it, temporarily supported on bricks so that it is just above the ground at the highest point and precisely level. Because the ground drops away, extra bricks will be needed at the lower end. If the panel is exactly level and the post vertical, the two should come together perfectly.

If U-shaped metal brackets are being used, these will either have been fixed to the post already or can be fixed just before the panel is offered up, so that the panel can be slid into position. The same sliding technique will apply if grooved concrete posts are being used. The panel will be fixed, at first temporarily, with a galvanized nail or two (timber posts). At this stage, the panel will be very vulnerable to wind and so will need steadying with a second pair of hands or a makeshift stay. The panel must be exactly in line with the string, as should the next post which is installed dead vertical with about 50 mm (2 in) protruding above the panel. If the ground has a significant slope downhill, this end of the panel may require a longer post than was first used, and this should be borne in mind when ordering the posts. If gravel boards are being used, set these into or on the ground before the panel is offered up and use them instead of piles of bricks to establish a precise level. Because a portion of this board could well end up below ground, it must be pressure treated or thoroughly painted with a preservative. Gravel boards are also used on perfectly level ground and are especially useful where the neighbour's ground is at a higher or lower level.

With the second post fixed into position, the first panel can be properly fixed or nailed before the panel is offered up in the same way, and so on. Finally, caps can be nailed to the post tops and perhaps capping strips fixed on to the tops of the panels. (Fig 13).

If it has not been possible to set the posts in as deeply as planned, it may be necessary to saw off their tops when the fence is all but finished. This is not a particularly easy task and care must be taken not to disturb the posts too much. If more preservative has to be painted on, then obviously any

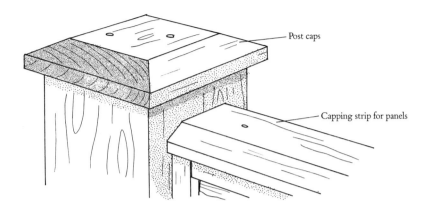

Fig. 13 Finishing off a panel fence.

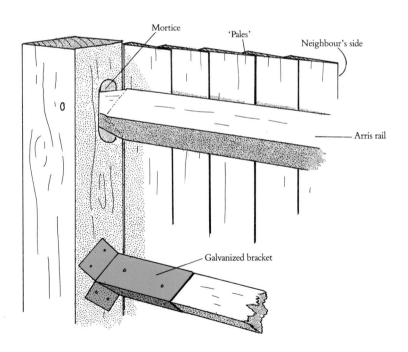

Fig. 14 Common methods of fixing together parts of a closeboard fence.

Although this would be an effective timber screen during the winter months, its summer appearance is very much enhanced by climbing roses and clematis. The horizontal wires allow the climbing plants to be well supported.

climbing plants must be kept away for as long as possible. If trellis is to be fixed on top of the fence, the posts will have to be correspondingly longer and the capping, normally fixed to the top of the panel, will go on top of the trellis instead.

CLOSE BOARD FENCING

This type of fencing is usually constructed from a 'kit' of components and requires just a little more skill than was involved with erecting a panel fence (Fig 14).

MATERIALS
The posts are about 150 mm (6 in) square in hard wood, eg oak (*Quercus robur*) or pressure treated soft woods. Cross bars called 'arris rails' are triangular in section while vertical 'pales' or featherboards are thicker down one edge than the other. Gravel boards of some sort – usually timber – are nearly always used and some form of capping can be fitted to the top of the finished fence. When ordering, one post and 29 (100 mm or 4 in) feather edge boards are needed for a section 2.4 m (8 ft) long, plus one extra post to finish off.

ERECTING THE MAIN FRAMEWORK
Set the posts into the ground using the same technique as for panel fencing. They can be bought with ready made mortice holes running right through and you will need to decide whether the posts need two, three or perhaps four of these. Fences over, say, 1.5 m (5 ft) may well have three and those over 2 m (6 ft 6 in) could well have four. The ends of the arris rails will have to be shaped so that they fit snugly into these holes. Alternatively, triangular metal brackets can be used to join arris rails to posts. Mortice holes are then not necessary.

Whichever method is used, two or three arris rails are offered up to the first, fixed post and, at the same time, the second post is positioned so that the other end of each arris rail can be supported or fixed. The bottom rail will be about 400 mm (16 in) up from the ground and the top rail about 225 mm (9 in) down from the top of the posts. On level ground, the arris rails will be fixed horizontally, but on a slope they would normally be fixed parallel to the general or average slope. This means, that, once adopted, the same slope would apply for as long as possible – at least until the ground levelled out or began to slope the opposite way. If mortice joints are used, the join is pinned with a galvanized nail or two once the rail has been firmly knocked home. Metal brackets are also nailed. There is not much to choose between fixing these brackets to the post first or to each end of the arris rail *before* fixing them to the posts. The rails must be parallel to each other and be so arranged that their back, flat edge is about 10 mm ($\frac{3}{8}$ in) in from the neighbour's side of the post.

CLADDING THE FRAMEWORK

Once the whole framework has been erected, set the gravel boards on or slightly into the ground between the posts. They must be positioned so that when the pales (featherboards) are nailed on to the back edge of the arris rails, the bottom end of each pale rests on top of the gravel board. The gravel boards are usually nailed to the posts.

The pales are then nailed on to the arris rails with galvanized nails. They must be absolutely vertical and overlap each other by about 12 mm $\frac{1}{2}$ in). If the fence slopes, there will be tiny wedges of light visible at the bottom of each pale where it rests on top of the gravel board. Because these pales are vertical and the gravel board slopes, they do in fact step down or up. At the top end of the pales, a line is usually stretched between the posts so that the pales can be neatly cut off parallel to the arris rails. This only applies to sloping fences, of course − not to those being constructed on flat sites.

FINISHING

If capping is needed all along the top of the fence, an extra square or rectangular section rail will have to be fixed on to the top of the pales so that there is something for the capping to be fixed to.

Ideally, the posts, rails and pales will have been pressure treated but if not, the whole fence will need painting or spraying with a preservative and/or a colour stain. This does not, however, apply to hardwoods eg oak (*Quercus robur*), which is simply left to season.

RUSTIC TRELLIS WORK

One form of screen which is relatively easy to construct and is not particularly expensive is rustic trellis work. There is a wide choice of timber but the more commonly used include pine, larch and sweet chestnut. They can all be obtained with their bark still intact but if they are pine or larch, this would indicate that these poles have not been pressure treated. The bark has to be removed to treat poles. Sweet chestnut is classed as a hardwood and does not really need treating, but larch and pine will not last long without treatment. It is therefore preferable to opt for treated timber for economic reasons.

SIZES OF POLES

The poles are measured across the top and main uprights, for example, ought to have a top diameter of 75–100 mm (3–4 in). Horizontal and diagonal poles will be thinner with 50–75 mm (2–3 in) tops. Other sizes can be used, too.

PLANNING A PATTERN

The necessary height, extent and position of the trellis should already have been decided upon, bearing in mind that the climbing plants which will eventually cover the trellis will add to the effective height, at least in summer. A pattern of uprights supporting a series of horizontal, vertical and perhaps diagonal timbers will need drawing to scale on paper. Then the sizes and numbers of poles can be worked out. The uprights will need to be set at least 400 mm (16 in) into the ground and preferably deeper.

NAILS AND TOOLS

Nails will be needed to fix the poles together. Galvanized nails sound sensible, but are unlikely to be available in large enough sizes. For this reason, ordinary steel nails with oval heads are generally used, mostly 100 mm (4 in) and 15 mm (6 in) long. A string line will again be needed together with a spirit level, claw hammer and a coarse-toothed panel saw. If a bow saw is used, the blade must be tightened up as far as it will go, or it could produce curved cuts. A spade or some other device will be needed to dig out the necessary holes.

CONSTRUCTION

First, put in the uprights along the required line, making sure they are as vertical as possible and sticking up out of the ground by the correct amount. It is rather difficult to judge with a spirit level whether they are vertical because the poles taper. If the two furthest end poles are put in first, a string line can be stretched very tightly between them and used to control the height of all the intermediate poles. It may sometimes be necessary to saw the tops of the poles down to the correct height, especially where it proves impossible to sink them any further into the ground. The best way to fix the posts into the ground is with well rammed hardcore, as for fence posts.

Generally speaking, trellis looks best with the horizontal cross bars mounted exactly level rather than sloping with the ground. A number of joints can be used to fix the various cross bars, some being quite complicated, but in practice just a few simple ones seem perfectly adequate (Fig 15). Fixing can be awkward since, unless work is planned carefully, nails end up in totally inaccessible corners and cannot be

This old wall could be rather harsh without its many trailing plants, many of which are probably thriving in the old lime mortar.

hammered home. A claw hammer is ideal for pulling out the bent nails. If a nail is bent on its way into the timber it is a waste of time trying to knock it straight again, because the bend is still there and the nail then takes the wrong path and perhaps protrudes where it is not wanted. All cut surfaces must be given a brushful of preservative because even pressure treatment does not always reach the very centre of a pole. Where tops of uprights have their cut surfaces exposed to the weather, it is a good idea to slope or chamfer these so that the rain can run off and not soak in too much. A water repellant preservative would be helpful. The sturdier the trellis is made, the better, since climbing plants will increase the risk of wind damage significantly and, in winter, heavy snow may collect on their branches. If the original design did not provide many timbers close to the ground, it may be necessary to add some, temporarily, to encourage the climbing plants upwards. One useful by-product of a rustic (or sawn timber) trellis is that thin chicken wire could be discreetly fixed to the bottom third or so to keep dogs or other animals in (or out). This will also provide perfect support for some of the smaller, less vigorous, climbers.

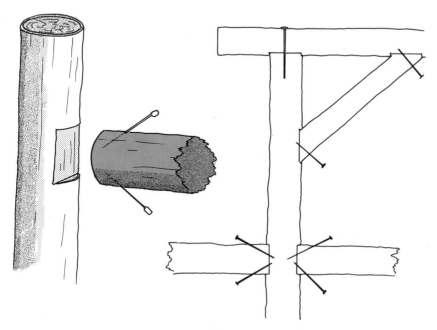

Fig. 15 Some simple joints for a rustic trellis work.

CHAPTER 4

PLANTS AS SCREENS

Because plants are living things, it takes quite a lot of skill to create a screen of predictable proportions. A few basic facts need to be considered to achieve a reasonable degree of success.

Most plants growing in a garden are allowed to grow to whatever size or shape they wish (within reason) and to take as long as necessary to do so. But as soon as plants are needed for a specific task, all this changes. Plants expected to form a screen must grow to about the right size and shape in a reasonably short space of time. This may have to be helped in a number of ways. It could require extra fertilizer, water, pruning and so on, but if the wrong type of plant is used in an unsuitable position in adverse soil conditions, the whole process could become almost impossible.

DIFFERENT TYPES OF PLANTS

Some plants make good hedges, others do not. If a slim, tight hedge is needed, plants with small leaves and frequently branching growth, yet which are not too rampant will have to be used. If, for example, sycamore (*Acer pseudoplatanus*) is used for a hedge, clipping would result in a lot of leaves being conspicuously cut in half and large gaps appearing generally. Growth would be relatively sparse and it would lose its leaves in winter. This plant is also a potential forest tree, so would be difficult to keep under control. In contrast the growth of *Lavandula spica* (lavender) is relatively slow and compact and responds well to clipping. Its main limitation would be a maximum height of about 1.2 m (4 ft).

There is still a place for forest trees, in a large natural shelter belt of trees where they are allowed to grow unhindered to their full size. One or two potentially large trees can be kept very small, especially beech (*Fagus sylvatica*), hornbeam (*Carpinus betulus*) and yew (*Taxus baccata*), but only because their leaves are comparatively small and when clipped they are able to produce many small branches. If left unclipped, they soon assume their natural forest proportions.

Some shrubs make good screens as long as they are not clipped or pruned too closely. A good example is the shrub rose which is often recommended for a screen or informal hedge. Provided there is at least 1.2 m (4 ft) of space for each plant, shrub roses can be very effective. But if they are sited where their width has to be constantly kept in check, then continual pruning could cut away many of the potential flowering shoots and defeat the object of that type of hedge.

Where plenty of width is available, a collection of trees, shrubs and conifers could, together, produce an interesting and varied screen, but this could look rather odd and less convincing if it has to be clipped back hard at some time.

Climbing plants are a natural choice where space is limited provided there is something for them to climb up. Unfortunately, many climbers are deciduous and even die back in severe weather. This means that hardy evergreen climbers are especially valuable.

CLIMATE

Climatic conditions have a part to play with all living screens. Some plants grow far more slowly in cold districts than in milder ones. An example is Escallonia, which can grow up to 2 m (6 ft 6 in) high as an informal screen or hedge where winter frosts are not too severe. In colder districts, the plants may be cut back by frost each winter, restricting its height to near 1 m (3 ft 3 in). Plants which are as sensitive as this are certainly unsuitable for windy situations where frost would almost certainly be accentuated during the winter. Only the toughest plants are suitable for windbreaks in these areas.

Sea air is often salt laden and restricts the choice still further to a relatively few plants which can resist salt in the air. Most plants appear 'burnt' if subjected to salty air.

LIGHT

Plants vary widely in their tolerance to light. Outdoor plants seldom fail completely if given too little or too much light but their general performance will be affected. If plants are being grown for a screen and rapid results are expected, then plants should be used which are compatible with the degree of light available. For example, if extra screening is needed beneath some tall trees where light is at a low level, Portugal laurel (*Prunus lusitancia*) will perform particularly well, whereas most conifers would be very poor. It is interesting to see that when a row of conifers extends under a canopy of trees their growth diminishes in proportion with the light and moisture. Here a different plant should be used where the tree canopy overhangs.

Some plants are still quite effective even where adverse light limits their performance. If variegated elder (*Sambucus nigra albovariegata*) is planted under trees, its growth may be only half that of plants out in the open, but its brightly variegated foliage will still be very attractive and its habit quite bushy.

Many plants produce less flowers in poor light. Wisteria, for example appears to flower best in a sunny position. When grown in the shade, few, if any, flowers appear, even though growth is just as vigorous. This brings its value into question since, without flowers, it is just an ordinary mass of greenery.

Unfortunately many books seem to adopt an uncompromising attitude on this subject, stating categorically that certain plants cannot be grown in such adverse conditions. This simply is not true of most of them, but where screening is needed, you may not wish to risk those that may only half succeed.

SOIL CONDITIONS

Since the choice of plants for screening is so wide, it must inevitably include some plants which are sensitive to acid or alkaline (chalky) soils. The most important point here is to realize that some plants will not grow well in chalky or alkaline soils and some may actually die. Plants belonging to the family *Ericaceae* are typical and must have acid soil. This includes rhododendrons, azaleas, pieris, heathers, pernettyas, kalmia and so on. Many of these plants are expensive to buy, so it is wise to test the soil before deciding which plants to use. A special kit containing test tubes and liquids, or a special meter will indicate whether the soil has a high pH (alkaline) or a low pH (acid).

$$\text{acid} \qquad\qquad \text{alkaline}$$
$$4.5 < \text{-------------------} > 7.0 < \text{-----------------} > 9$$
$$\text{neutral}$$

Fortunately, most plants are not too sensitive and those which show only a slight sensitivity (preferring acid soil, like some magnolias) can be helped by being planted with a good deal of moist peat around their roots, or by being fed sequestered iron from time to time. Waterlogged soil will slow down the growth of many plants (including most conifers) but a few trees and shrubs, especially willows (*Salix*), alders (*Alnus*) and dogwoods (*Cornus*) prefer wet or damp soil. Watering plants at least

Opposite: This mixture of trees, shrubs and conifers provides one of the most attractive types of plant screens where space is available. Many of these plants are evergreen.

during their first summer will ensure the best possible growth, especially under large trees, but it could take plants several seasons to settle in and grow at their maximum rate. All plants respond to feeding and an occasional dressing of a general fertilizer will help to maintain their growth. Feeding significantly increases the growth of old tired hedges and screens which have been pruned hard back to regenerate them.

BUYING PLANTS

Putting aside value for money, which is very difficult to quantify in the pages of a book, there are some points to note before actually buying plants. Trees and shrubs are sold in different ways.

Shrubs and conifers are sold as:

Nursery liners – very small, and intended to be grown on in a nursery but may be available as cheap, small specimens and are often sold by mail order.
Container grown – in pots or bags. They vary in size but can be bought and planted at any time of the year.
Open ground, root balled – dug up from a nursery field during the dormant season. The ball of roots, especially of conifers, is wrapped in netting or hessian. The netting can sometimes be left on when planting so the roots are not disturbed.
Open ground, with bare roots – again dug from the ground in the dormant season but with the roots left naked, sometimes with very little soil. Plants bought like this must be protected from drying out and planted as soon as possible.

Trees are sold in the same way but come in a variety of sizes (Fig 16).

The ideal planting time for bare root and root balled plants is in the autumn when the soil is still warm enough to stimulate new root growth. Root growth tends to continue unless the ground becomes frozen, so that by the spring they can cope with the sudden demands placed upon them.

On poorly managed nurseries, root balled (and even containerized) plants may harbour perennial weeds. Unfortunately, many of these weeds are not visible in winter when the plants are likely to be bought and so are not discovered until it is too late. This problem can be partly averted by visiting the nursery during the summer to make sure the plants are free from weeds.

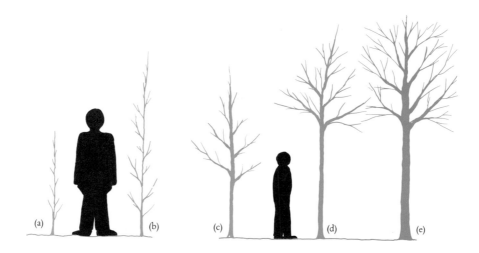

Fig. 16 Common tree sizes. The smallest trees available are (*a*) whips, and (*b*) feathered. Larger trees are available as (*c*) half standards, (*d*) full standards, and (*e*) extra heavy nursery stock.

Well grown plants will usually show smooth, vigorous straight growth with healthy foliage. A poor nursery will display more stunted plants with tatty leaves – the result of erratic watering and little or no feeding. A trip around several nurseries and plant centres will enable you to make some sort of comparison and help in the difficult task of getting value for money.

PLANTING

Since the heart of a plant is its root system, the more vigorous the roots are, the quicker the top grows. The performance of any hedge or screen therefore depends, at least initially, on the way in which it has been planted. In most instances, the bigger the planting hole the better, especially if the native soil is very poor. One very important factor is that the plant must not be planted any deeper than it was growing in its pot or on the nursery. The following description covers the planting and staking of a bare-rooted standard tree. The technique is basically the same for conifers and shrubs, though a stake may not be necessary.

Dig a hole about 20 cm (8 in) wider than the root system. If any of the roots are damaged, then these portions should be removed with secateurs. The hole can be as deep as required, perhaps down to 90 cm (3 ft) in very poor or stony soil. Keep the topsoil separate from the subsoil so that the former can be re-used and the latter discarded.

If planting in grass or a lawn, a circle or square of turf will need to be taken up first. A sheet of polythene will also help to keep the soil separate from the lawn. Well rotted compost (free from perennial weeds), old farmyard manure or peat can be forked into the base of the hole. This will help to hold moisture during the summer and improve drainage as well as encourage deeper root penetration. Some of the topsoil can also be mixed with compost and put back into the hole. The level in the hole should be built back up and firmed so that the tree roots will be just the

Fig. 17 A common type of tree tie and spacer.

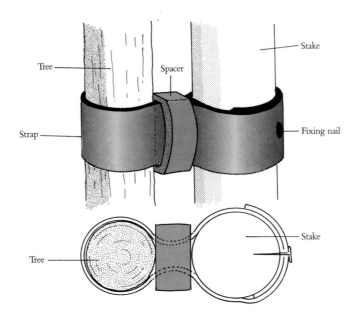

Shrubs and climbing plants can be mixed to produce an attractive screen with all the year round interest.

right level when placed upon it. At this stage, with the tree held temporarily in position, a metal or wood tree stake can be positioned to pass between the major roots, close to the stem and miss any branches. With the tree removed the stake can be knocked firmly in. If it is still too high and likely to rub on branches, a portion can be sawn from the top of a wooden post. The tree is now replaced with more moist peat and soil piled on top of the roots. By jerking the whole tree up and down a few times, soil will settle down between all the roots. More soil is added before all is well firmed with the heel of your boot.

Planting must always be firm, so the soil and compost must be firmed thoroughly at all stages before and after positioning the tree. The tree should finish at the same depth as it was in the nursery. One or two ties will be needed to fix the tree to its stake, incorporating spacers so that the stem or branches do not rub on the stake (Fig 17). Never pile up the soil around the base of the tree like a mole hill. In lawns, the soil in the hole should be about 3.5 cm ($1\frac{1}{2}$ in) below the surface of the turf so that rain-water can collect.

Although it is usually assumed that a tree needs a stake mainly to stop it from blowing over in the wind, stakes can be helpful in other ways. They keep conifers growing straight and ensure that roots do not rock about while the fragile but vital root hairs are developing underground. Further protection may be needed on exceptionally windy sites, a matter which is covered under 'windbreaks'.

CHAPTER 5

HEDGES

There are two basic types of hedge — formal and informal. The first is clipped regularly and can, as a result, be kept quite narrow and down to a precise height. An informal hedge relies much more on the natural shape of the plant and is often left unclipped most of the time. Many of these plants, however, are grown partly for their flowers which tend to form on the ends of shoots. These can be cut back after flowering.

WHICH TYPE OF HEDGE TO HAVE

As with any man-made screen, the height and position of a hedge will need working out beforehand. The first consideration is whether the hedge is to be deciduous or evergreen, since this narrows the choice straight away.

WIDTH AND HEIGHT
It does not necessarily follow that a tall hedge has to be wide but hedges which are clipped regularly must be shaped for stability — wider at the base than at the top. Some of the narrowest hedges are formed by conifers while informal hedges are nearly always relatively wide and not especially tall. Table 5.1 highlights this, though the five-year-old dimensions are only approximate.

GENERAL APPEARANCE
Hedges come in a variety of colours with green, of course, being the most common. Even this varies widely from the lightish green of griselinia to the very dark and sombre yew (*Taxus*). Although foliage provides the main source of colour many informal hedges (and a few formal ones) produce flowers which influence the overall effect for at least part of the year. Beech (*Fagus sylvatica*) is rather unusual in that it offers brown leaves all winter in more sheltered localities. The colour of a hedge can influence the choice of plant to be set in front of it. Pink and white roses can look particularly attractive in front of a purple hedge; purple or golden foliage can look striking in front of a dark green hedge, and so on.

Above: This illustrates how narrow a conifer hedge can be kept if trimmed regularly and from an early age.

Opposite: Forsythia can be kept as a remarkably neat hedge and is especially valuable for its very early flowers.

Table 5.1 Different types of hedges

Plant	Height in 5 yrs	Width	Shape	Evergreen or Deciduous
Berberis × *stenophylla*	1.2 m (4 ft)	1.2 m (4 ft) unclipped		evergreen
Carpinus betulus (hornbeam) and *Crataegus monogyna* (hawthorn) and *Fagus sylvatica* (beech)	1.5 m (5 ft)	37.5 cm (15 in) clipped		deciduous
Chamaecyparis lawsoniana 'Columnaris'	2.4 m (8 ft)	45 cm (18 in) clipped		evergreen
× *Cupressocyparis leylandii*	2.7 m (9 ft)	60 cm (2 ft) clipped		evergreen

Name	Height	Spacing		Type
Escallonia (in mild districts)	1.2 m (4 ft)	90 cm (3 ft) unclipped		mainly evergreen
Ilex aquifolium (holly)	1.2 m (4 ft)	37.5 cm (15 in) clipped		evergreen
Ligustrum	2.1 m (7 ft)	45 cm (18 in) clipped		semi-evergreen
Rosa rugosa hybrids (shrub rose)	1.5 m (5 ft)	1.2 m (4 ft) unclipped		deciduous
Taxus baccata (yew)	1.2 m (4 ft)	37.5 cm (15 in) clipped		evergreen

The following lists give some ideas on hedge colours.
(E = Evergreen   S/E = Semi-evergreen)

Dark green

Cupressocyparis leylandii (conifer)	E
Fagus sylvatica (beech)	
Ilex aquifolium (holly)	E
Prunus laurocerasus (laurel)	E
Prunus lusitanica (Portugal laurel)	E
Taxus baccata (yew)	E

Pale Green

Chamaecyparis lawsoniana 'Pottenii' (conifer)	E
Forsythia spectabilis	
Griselinia littoralis	E

Yellow, Golden or Variegated

Berberis thunbergii 'Aurea' (unclipped)	
Chamaecyparis lawsoniana 'Lanei' (and others)	E
Cupressocyparis leylandii 'Castlewellan'	E
Forsythia spectabilis (flowers) (clipped)	E
Griselinia variegata	E
Ligustrum ovalifolium 'Aureum' (golden privet)	S/E
Philadelphus coronarius 'Aureus' (mock orange) (unclipped)	
Prunus lusitanica 'Variegata'	E
Taxus baccata 'Aurea' (golden yew)	E

Purple

Berberis × *ottawensis* 'Purpurea'	
Berberis thunbergii 'Atropurpurea'	
Cotinus coggygria 'Royal Purple' unclipped (broad)	
Fagus sylvatica purpurea (purple beech)	
Prunus 'Cistena' (purple-leaved cherry)	
Rosa rubrifolia (unclipped)	

Grey/Silver

Atriplex halimus (unclipped)	
Elaeagnus angustifolia (clipped or unclipped)	E
Eucalyptus gunnii (clipped)	E
Hippophae rhamnoides (unclipped)	S/E
Lavandula (lavender) small, clipped or unclipped	E

This hedge of *Berberis stenophylla* should not be pruned until its early summer flowering has finished.

Leaf size is also important. Hedges with large leaves, like cherry laurel (*Prunus laurocerasus*) can appear very neat when viewed at a distance but, close up, are not as effective as something with small leaves like yew (*Taxus*). Yew can also be trimmed to intricate shapes, as in topiary.

HEDGE TRIMMING

Informal hedges can be cut back with a hedge trimmer or secateurs. Where individual branches are cut back, perhaps when removing dead flowers, secateurs are best. This provides an opportunity to cut branches accurately, so that each ends in a bud or leaf (Fig 18).

If the branches are very small and numerous, secateurs will take too long, so shears or powered hedge trimmers are more appropriate. In many ways the latter are far more effective on formal hedges where an overall smooth finish is required but formal hedges that have become overgrown may have to be cut with secateurs or even a saw to start with. It does not matter which type of secateurs is used, so long as they are sharp. Shears with smooth blades are adequate for hedges with thin shoots but thicker shoots will simply slip out as the shears are closed. Shears with one or more notches along at least one blade are necessary for cutting thicker shoots.

Fig. 18 Pruning with secateurs means that each branch can be properly cut back to a bud.

Table 5.2 Frequency of cutting for neat, formal hedges.
Hedging plants which need trimming:

every three to four weeks during summer:
Ligustrum ovalifolium (privet)
Lonicera nitida

two or three times during summer:
Buxus sempervirens (box)
Conifers (most types)
Carpinus betulus (hornbeam)
Fagus sylvatica (beech)
Taxus baccata (yew)

just once or twice:
Crataegus (hawthorn)
Lavandula (lavender). More frequent trimming will prevent flowering
Prunus laurocerasus (laurel)

Hedge trimmers need to be as light as possible. Electric cables are always a hazard, so it is essential to use a safety circuit breaker in conjunction with the cable. Rechargeable hedge trimmers overcome this problem but may not be so light to handle. Trimming is supposed to start at the bottom of the hedge and work upwards, so that the trimmings fall clear and do not become hitched up on uncut branches. This is quite important for formal hedges but not quite so critical for informal ones especially where secateurs are being used. Scaffolding will be needed to trim the tops of tall and wide hedges. If a hedge is likely to need frequent trimming, this is going to be a recurring problem, so it would be wise either to choose a plant which needs only one or two cuts a year, or to restrict the height of the hedge so that something less elaborate than scaffolding can be used.

When a hedge needs only one trim each year, it is usually best to cut it as soon as the main flush of growth has finished and hardened up. With hawthorn (*Crataegus*) for example, this might be in the latter half of the summer. There is a good chance that, cut this late, it will not regrow significantly before the winter. However, it does mean that this hedge will look untidy for some weeks beforehand. Conversely, an informal hedge which produces flowers on the ends of the new shoots will need cutting as soon as flowering has finished so that there is time for new shoots to grow (eg *Berberis* × *stenophylla*).

Above: A rose hedge should always be given plenty of space to develop informally.

Opposite: The height and attractiveness of this lavender hedge has been increased by the use of a compact and contrasting bush rose.

The more frequently formal hedges are trimmed, especially conifers and privet (*Ligustrum*), the tighter the growth becomes. Conifer hedges need particularly regular *light* trimming in their early years to encourage a tight branch system. All too often young conifers are left untrimmed until they are perhaps 45 cm (18 in) across, which leads to an even wider hedge in later years. It is quite possible to keep even a good sized conifer hedge down to a width of 45 cm (18 in) if light trimming is started early. Evergreen hedges, especially conifers, are better not cut in frosty weather since there is a danger of the cut ends going brown.

The tops of hedging conifers must be left uncut until the thicker part of the conifer has reached the desired height. By this time, the leading wisp of growth – the terminal shoot – could be as much as 90 cm (3 ft) above this.

TOPIARY

Topiary is the art of creating figures and patterns from hedging plants. In recent years, the use of topiary seems to have declined, perhaps because people seldom live in one place long enough to achieve anything. Creating figures and shapes from plant material does take time. It requires a plant with strong yet supple branches, and relatively small leaves to create the detail. Yew (*Taxus*) is ideal but other plants could be considered, among them privet (*Ligustrum*). Some branches are allowed to develop freely from the top of the plant until they are large enough to manipulate. With careful pruning and even some wiring, a basic shape can be started. Through constant pruning and clipping, the detail of the shape is encouraged to develop.

Wiring can be done by wrapping stiff copper wire in a spiral around supple stems, then bending the stems to shape. The wire holds the stem in position until the stem thickens and stiffens to some extent. Wires wrapped around in spring will need checking and possibly re-adjusting by the following autumn. If this is not done, the wires can eat into the stems and cause permanent damage. Eventually the branches will hold their shape and tufts of growth can be encouraged to form the bulk of the figure. Arches as well as holes or windows in hedges can be created in a similar manner.

PLANTING HEDGES

The technique described for tree planting can still apply, except that a stake may not be needed. Spacing will vary according to the type of plant, and how rapidly a dense screen is needed. Planting distances can be assessed by visiting a nursery and looking at various hedging plants at different ages. With conifers in particular a nursery which grows them in the open ground may well have each type in different sizes, so that it can be judged how wide each plant is likely to be in, say, another couple of years time. Older plants will be found in other people's gardens. As a rough example, plants of × *Cupressocyparis leylandii* planted at 60cm (2ft) centres will probably form a dense screen within three years. At 90cm (3ft) centres they could well take five years. Plants of laurel (*Prunus laurocerasus*) planted at 90cm (3ft) centres could well form quite a dense screen in three years. For the narrowest formal hedges, including those of conifers, plants will need to be set fairly close together in a *single* row.

Wider formal hedges of plants like hawthorn (*Crataegus*), beech (*Fagus*), hornbeam (*Carpinus*) and laurel (*Prunus laurocerasus*) can be planted in two rows, staggered in a zig-zag line. As a result the hedge will be denser and wider. In windy situations, the plants can be tied to wires stretched tightly between temporary posts for the first year or two. Some people are of the opinion that plants which are permanently supported in some way never fully develop the ability to stand unaided later in life and may succumb to gales or snow damage. This applies to trees as well as hedges. Evergreen hedges must be avoided where they might be within reach of cattle, as many evergreens, particularly yew (*Taxus*), are poisonous.

MIXED HEDGES

In some instances, a mix of two or more different plants can be used to create a hedge. The various plants used for strictly formal hedges need to be of about the same vigour, or results can be patchy, though this can be evened up to some extent by clipping. 'Country' hedges which are traditionally less precise, may have wild roses, honeysuckle and clematis added to the main plant but this does create difficulties with pruning. The main plant might need pruning or clipping just when the roses and honeysuckle are at their best.

RECLAIMING OLD HEDGES

A hedge may already exist in a neglected garden, though it has long since reverted from a neat, formal affair to an unacceptable mess. Most hedges (except conifers) will respond to hard pruning by producing a profusion

of new growth. Cutting may have to be done with a saw and some caution is advisable if the very oldest, central wood is cut into. Buds which have not been called upon to grow for many years may no longer have the potential to do so. It is difficult to predict how they will react since it seems to depend upon the individual circumstances rather than the species. The safest and most sensible approach is to ascertain where the hedge always used to be trimmed. This is usually obvious from the way in which a particular zone in the hedge appears to have developed smaller, closely knit branches, before growing out of hand. The hedge is more likely to produce a neat result quickly when cut back to this point.

Farm hedges of hawthorn (*Crataegus*), field maple (*Acer campestre*), hazel (*Corylus*) and so on can be 'laid'. Branches are partially cut through with a small hatchet type tool so that they can be laid down in the hedge. Sometimes virtually all the branches are treated this way. Every so often, vertical sticks can be inserted or vertical branches left uncut, producing a woven effect, almost like a wattle hurdle. Because the branches are still attached, they produce growth which, as a result of the laying, forms a dense, cattle-proof barrier. Eventually, after a number of years, the process may have to be repeated.

Old conifer hedges or screens will seldom respond to hard pruning. They are best pruned lightly, keeping within the younger growth zone. Once they have become too old and patchy, they really need to be taken out completely to make room for a new hedge.

Opposite: This neat screen of conifers (*Cupressocyparis leylandii* 'Castlewellan'), is hiding the garden compost bin.

CHAPTER 6

WINDBREAKS AND TALL SCREENS

The most effective solution for a windbreak is a rather unlikely one. The secret of success is to slow down the wind or filter it. To stop it altogether is a recipe for disaster. For this reason, only certain types of screens and plants are suitable. Fig 19 shows how windbreaks work. A solid barrier only makes matters worse or moves the problem on somewhere else. It can also be seen from the diagram that the height of a windbreak bears a relationship to the size of area protected. Manufactured screens or screen block walls are ideal for sheltering small areas like patios where people will benefit as much as plants.

Where a large area of garden needs sheltering, plant screens are often a more realistic proposition, offering greater height – though probably at the expense of rather valuable space. Vegetables grow better in sheltered conditions but must have as much light and moisture as possible, so they should not be so close to a tall plant screen that they are constantly starved of both. The pollination of fruit also depends upon relatively protected conditions in which bees and other insects can move around pollinating unhindered. Again, overshadowing by a windbreak should be avoided.

Bear in mind that a tall screen of trees can have considerable root spread and this is especially so with poplars, which have the greatest spread of all. At the height of the growing season, they will absorb considerable amounts of moisture and nutrients so that any plants nearby do not get their fair share. Also, a tall, living screen can shade quite a large area of garden, although in a very sunny situation this may not be a bad thing. All of this means that living screens are really only suitable for large gardens.

In a small garden, where a plant screen would be on top of the crops, a man-made screen might be a better proposition. But on large estates there could be room for a very substantial screen of trees and conifers growing a safe distance from sensitive crops. An extensive area could be protected by this screen.

Table 6.1 Plants suitable for large windbreaks

Acer platanoides (Norway maple) including the purple-leaved version.
Acer pseudoplatanus (sycamore) including the purple-leaved version.
Alnus incana (alder) – especially in wet areas.
Betula pendula (birch) – planted in thickets.
Chamaecyparis lawsoniana (Lawson cypress) – dense, though not
　　particularly fast.
× *Cupressocyparis leylandii* (including golden 'Castlewellan' – very fast.
Pinus nigra and other tall-growing pines.
Populus alba (white poplar)
Populus nigra 'Italica' – Lombardy poplar.
Quercus ilex (evergreen oak) – rather slow.
Salix alba (willow) – including several with coloured winter stems.
　　Ideal in wet areas.

Best planted in staggered rows with about 28 m – 2.4 m (6 ft 6 in – 8 ft) between plants but closer if rapid results are needed.

MANUFACTURED WINDBREAKS

Apart from all the various screens described earlier in the book, various plastic nettings are available. Most are in the form of webbing which gives perhaps 50% screening from the wind.

Their height is limited, perhaps up to 3 m (9 ft 9 in) and reasonably strong supports (maybe with cross wires) will be necessary. This webbing could be used as a temporary measure to screen some types of plants which are trying to establish a more permanent windbreak nearby. Another, more permanent arrangement is to mount thin wooden laths horizontally or vertically on a strong wooden frame so that they provide about 50% protection.

PROTECTING YOUNG CONIFERS

A conifer hedge can be particularly prone to frost damage when the ground is frozen. With the roots frozen and dormant, the wind can suck moisture out of the foliage and damage it beyond recovery. A temporary webbing screen can be very helpful in districts where this is a problem. Another way of achieving this protection, without a screen, is to spray the conifers with an anti-transpirant at the beginning of the winter. This

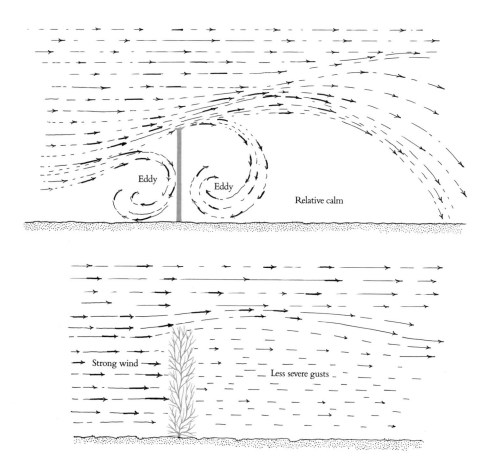

Fig. 19 *Above:* A solid barrier stops the wind completely but can create severe and damaging gusts. *Below:* A partial barrier slows down and disperses strong winds more effectively.

is a clear liquid plastic which coats the foliage and prevents it from losing too much moisture. The same product can be used to stop Christmas trees from losing their needles indoors. The product should be used according to the manufacturer's instructions which will be found on the can. The alternative is to spray newly planted conifers daily with plain water.

This screen of wooden laths will filter and slow down the wind but would be less effective if allowed to become covered by climbing plants.

FROST HOLLOWS

On sloping ground where the air is cold and still, air gradually moves downhill. If a hedge or screen completely blocks its path, the air builds up like water behind a dam until it finally spills over the top. As the night wears on, the air trapped by the hedge becomes colder until frost forms. This is known as a frost pocket and the process can be seen very clearly as mists moving about on farmland and spilling over hedges. The resulting frost can obviously damage plants, especially vegetables and fruit blossom. This problem can be eased by leaving a gap in the hedge or screen so that the cold air can flow out, but this may be impossible to arrange if the screen is on neighbouring land.

SHELTER BY THE SEA

As mentioned earlier, there are screens of plastic or glass. As solid screens, these have a very localized effect and could hardly be expected to shelter a whole garden. All the 'manufactured' screens are applicable but salt spray will still penetrate them and limit the variety of plants which can be used. Very often, gardeners who live by the sea choose to have a living screen comprised of wind- and salt-resistant shrubs or trees, of which there are many, as shown in the Table 6.2. One of the most widely used trees is the evergreen oak, *Quercus ilex*, and this has been used to shelter some well known coastal gardens on the west coast of Scotland. Among the shrubs, the sea buckthorn, *Hippophae rhamnoides*, is often used and makes a very effective screen in the smaller garden. So, too, does tamarix, a typical maritime shrub.

OTHER TALL SCREENS

Man-made screens are usually very limited in height but one, not previously mentioned, does tend to reach higher than most – a chain link fence. On its own, it does little to slow down the wind but coupled with some vigorous climbing plants, it can be quite successful. A chain link fence can, with suitable supports, extend upwards to 3 m (9 ft 9 in) or even higher. Climbing plants like Virginia creeper (*Parthenocissus*), Russian vine (*Polygonum baldschuanicum*), honeysuckle (*Lonicera*), some types of climbing rose and various ivies (*Hedera*) will provide cover up to this height quite readily. More exotic plants should be reserved for more sheltered positions against walls and small trellises.

Table 6.2 Plants for screens close to the sea
TREES
Acer pseudoplatanus (sycamore) and its various cultivars
Crataegus – hawthorn
Populus alba (poplars) and others
Quercus ilex (evergreen oak)
Salix – most willows
Sorbus aria – whitebeam
Sorbus intermedia – mountain ash
Ilex aquifolium – holly. It may scorch in severe conditions

SHRUBS
Arundinaria – bamboos
Atriplex
Berberis – mostly deciduous types
Elaeagnus – especially *E. ebbingei*
Escallonia
Euonymus ovatus
Hebes – most types unless the climate is very cold
Hippophaë – sea buckthorn
Ligustrum – privet
Pyracantha – firethorn
Rosa rugosa
Sambucus nigra and others – elder
Senecio – various
Symphoricarpos – snowberry
Tamarix
Ulex – gorse

It may be possible to grow a much wider range of plants in a seaside garden if screens are used but it is usually a matter of trial and error.

CHAPTER 7

PLANTS FOR WALLS, FENCES AND INFORMAL SCREENING

There are three main categories of wall plants:

a) those which attach themselves with tendrils or by twining around something
b) others which attach themselves using sucker pads
c) mostly shrubby plants which readily grow against and up walls (and fences).

PLANTS AGAINST BUILDINGS

Plants of any sort against a building tend to arouse suspicion that some structural damage is inevitable. It would certainly be inadvisable to grow sucker type plants against rendered, decorated surfaces since, at the very least, it would prove difficult to re-decorate. But, more seriously, the extra weight of the plants could eventually dislodge the rendering. Old brick buildings with soft lime mortar might also be a poor choice for such plants since there is some evidence that the sucker pads could loosen the mortar. This is much less likely to occur where the mortar is new and hard with cement.

Plants growing near or against walls are only likely to encourage dampness if the stem is so close that soil and wet leaves build up between it and the wall above the damp course. Most of the time and almost always with evergreen shrubs, walls are kept drier by the canopy of leaves, rather than the opposite.

Problems can occur where very vigorous climbers or shrubs are planted very close to walls. As the stems thicken, pressure might be exerted on the wall. Vines and wisteria can be particularly troublesome, so these should be planted away from the wall to allow for expansion. If

Table 7.1 Different types of climbing plants

Plants which adhere to walls with sucker pads
Hedera – all types of ivy
Hydrangea petiolaris – climbing hydrangea
Parthenocissus – Virginia creepers
Pileostegia viburnoides – an evergreen climber with creamy white flowers

Plants with tendrils or twisting leaf stalks
Ampelopsis – similar to Parthenocissus but sometimes bears ornamental fruits
Passiflora – passion flower
Vitis – various vines, ornamental and edible
Clematis – all types
Eccremocarpus scaber – half-hardy climber with scarlet flowers
Smilax – a handsome evergreen

Plants with twining stems
Actinidia kolomikta – some leaves have pink tips
Akebia quinata – semi-evergreen with attractive foliage
Aristolochia – Dutchman's pipe
Celastrus orbiculatus – has curious orange-yellow fruits
Humulus lupulus 'Aureus' – golden hop
Jasminum officinale – summer jasmine
Lonicera – honeysuckles
Polygonum baldschuanicum – Russian vine
Solanum crispum 'Glasnevin' – has blue 'potato' flowers
Solanum jasminoides – white 'potato' flowers
Wisteria floribunda 'Macrobotrys' – an exceptionally large-flowered wisteria

---

an adjacent building has no proper foundations nor solid floors, some wall plants may grow under the wall and up into the house. Wisteria and Virginia creeper (*Parthenocissus*) have been known to do this. Large wall plants which span several floors have been known to help mice and squirrels up to the bedrooms and insects certainly enjoy the cover these plants provide. Despite all this, there are many situations where plants are especially welcome against walls covering a variety of situations and, of course, most of the problems just described do not apply to free-standing garden walls, fences or trellis.

THE BEST ASPECT

Plants growing against walls or fences have to rely on light reaching them from only one or two directions, rather than from all round as plants do on an open trellis or in an island bed. It is therefore quite important to choose a suitable aspect for plants which may not produce the very feature they have been grown for in adverse conditions, like the wisteria, described earlier.

Early spring flowering plants like camellia, for example, might have its flowers thawed out too quickly on a frosty morning if the early sun were to catch them. The flowers would then turn brown. This is more likely to happen against a house wall than a bungalow wall because the latter has lower and often wider eaves, which offer a good measure of protection at least from radiation frost. Plants which resent frost might be best in a sheltered corner which receives sun for much of the day. The wall absorbs the heat during the day and releases it at night, giving the plant some protection from frost. Fences do not hold the heat nearly so well and are not suitable for the more tender plants in cold districts.

Clematis seem to resent their roots becoming hot and dry but will be quite happy if their roots are in the shade but their branches are in the full sun. Japanese flowering quince (*Chaenomeles speciosa*) appears to flower and grow well on any aspect, as do pyracantha and winter-flowering jasmine (*Jasminum nudiflorum*). Other plants defy all reason, performing well in one garden and not in another, despite being given the same conditions. Generally speaking, plants which seem to do well on shady walls also do well on walls receiving early morning sun (except in the circumstances mentioned earlier) and plants which prefer a sunny aspect are usually successful on walls which receive afternoon and evening sun.

WALL FIXINGS

Plants with tendrils or which climb by twisting around things need something to help them. Trellis work is ideal but bare walls need something extra. The least obvious support on bare brick walls is galvanized wire stretched horizontally in line with the mortar joints every three or four courses. Fixing each end will have to be firm and rust proofed, using size ten to fourteen screws or screwed 'eyes' into plastic wall plugs.

Wall plugs may pull out where mortar is very soft, but this can be averted if some of the old mortar is scraped out (reasonably deeply) and new mortar trowelled in. While the new mortar is still soft, wall plugs can be pushed in so that they are gripped firmly when the mortar sets.

On decorated, rendered walls, plastic-covered steel or timber trellis can be hung on strong hooks. This provides a less permanent arrangement in which the trellis, complete with its plant can be unhooked and laid on the ground while redecorating takes place. Special wall nails can be used which have a lead tag. The nails are banged straight into a mortar joint and the lead tag is wrapped around the stem of a plant. These will be needed in quite large numbers if the plant is rampant but fewer for wall shrubs which just need steadying here and there.

Heavy trellis work, used as a permanent fixture will need fixing with expanding wall bolts rather than the lighter wall plugs. Wall bolts require larger holes and are usually fixed very precisely into the wall so that the trellis frame can be offered up and pushed on to them before being secured with nuts. As expanding wall bolts can lift the top few courses of brickwork, perhaps close to the eaves of the house, to be on the safe side, the top five or six courses of brickwork should be left alone.

Similar ideas can be applied to fences and, of course, fixing is usually easier. It is, perhaps, more important to use a removable system here, to allow for the use of timber preservatives. It could be impossible to fix things to walls or fences which belong to somebody else or on to metal objects like oil and gas tanks, so free-standing trellis, or wire stretched between free-standing posts, will then have to be used.

Plants which attach themselves by suckers are usually quite self-sufficient but may need some encouragement during the first few months. This can be provided with pieces of weather resistant sticky tape on to the wall or a small nail and some thin wire on a fence.

A SELECTION OF PLANTS FOR WALLS
MOSTLY IN SHADE

Azara microphylla – An evergreen shrub with very small leaves. In early spring, tiny, yellow, subtly scented flowers appear, partly hidden by the foliage. It will need tying back and can be very vulnerable to snow damage (not always hardy).

Chaenomeles speciosa – A thorny, deciduous shrub, often given the name 'quince' or 'japonica'. Scarlet, pink or white flowers are produced in spring before the leaves and to a lesser extent, during the summer. Although it can be kept quite neat by pruning, it is vigorous and should not be planted right at the edge of a path. The border needs to be at least 60 cm (2 ft) wide. (Fully hardy).

Clematis – Nearly all the large-flowered clematis will succeed, though, given the chance, they will try to reach a part of the wall that receives some sun. The disease called clematis wilt can strike this plant down in its prime and is so prevalent in some districts that it is then better to regard the clematis as a short-stay visitor than as a permanent one. The small-flowered clematis, *Clematis montana*, prefers a sunnier position where it will flower prolifically in spring. (Hardy).

Euonymus fortunei – A self-clinging evergreen with small, often brightly variegated leaves. With some encouragement it will climb upwards to cover a wall several metres high. (Hardy).

Forsythia suspensa – A rather untidy, loose growing forsythia which needs plenty of tying back in a confined space. The flowers are not always prolific but are quite large and showy. (Hardy).

Garrya elliptica – An evergreen wall shrub with very dark green, almost matt leaves. It can be kept quite neat with secateurs but care is needed because any winter pruning could remove the shoots which produce long, greyish green segmented catkins in early spring. (Quite hardy).

Hedera (ivy) – All manner of hederas, which are self clinging, are at home on a shady wall. In such dull conditions, the variegated cultivars are the most valuable. In colder districts *Hedera canariensis* 'Variegata' may not be hardy. An alternative would be *Hedera colchica dentata* 'Variegata'. (Most hederas are hardy). All should be trimmed back hard in early spring each year to prevent them becoming excessively heavy.

Hydrangea petiolaris – Deciduous, self-clinging leafy hydrangea which produces whitish flowers during the summer. The leaves fall to expose attractive papery brown stems in winter. (Hardy).

Jasminum nudiflorum – A semi-evergreen winter-flowering jasmine with distinctive green stems and, in early spring, yellow flowers. It may become rather untidy and top heavy and consequently needs to be well supported on wires or trellis. (Hardy). It makes a very attractive companion for *Garrya elliptica*, described above.

Opposite: This collection of mixed *Pyracantha* would be ideal for a north or east facing wall and is mainly evergreen.

Lonicera japonica repens 'Aureoreticulata' – A variegated honey-suckle which is grown more for its yellow-veined leaves than for its flowers. (Hardy).

Parthenocissus – Commonly known as Virginia creeper. These are grown mainly for their brilliant orange and red autumn colouring but are deciduous, self-clinging and often invasive. The leaf shape varies with the cultivar but all are rather similar. One of the best for autumn colour is *Parthenocissus tricuspidata* 'Veitchii'. (Hardy).

Polygonum baldschuanicum – Often known as 'Russian vine' or 'mile-a-minute vine'. It is deciduous and rampantly untidy, needing frequent tying back to wires if it is to be contained. It seems happiest hanging over fences and sheds. Although it grows rampantly on a shady wall it may not always produce such an abundance of its creamy white flowers as it would in full sun. (Very hardy).

Pyracantha – A mainly evergreen, thorny shrub which can be kept neat with a pair of secateurs or even shears. In late spring it opens clusters of creamy white flowers which are followed by orange, red or yellow berries in autumn. Birds eventually eat the berries (except, sometimes, the yellow ones). (Hardy).

There are lots of varieties of pyracantha, popularly known as firethorn. *P. angustifolia* has orange-yellow berries which persist throughout winter. The deep yellow berries of *P. atalantioides* 'Flava' are generally left alone by the birds. Very popular on account of its very heavy crops of large orange-red berries is *P. coccinea* 'Lalandei'. There are lots of named pyracantha hybrids available. Here's a selection: 'Golden Charmer', orange-yellow berries; 'Mohave', orange-red; 'Orange Charmer' and 'Orange Glow', deep orange berries. *P. rogersiana* 'Flava' is a well known yellow-berried firethorn.

Climbing roses – 'Golden Showers' (yellow) and 'Danse du Feu' (orange-red) are two examples of roses which will flower well without sun. They must be trained on wires or trellis. (Hardy).

As well as the popular varieties, there are many more climbing roses which will flourish and flower well on shady, e.g. north-facing, walls. Here is a selection of well known modern, repeat-flowering varieties: 'Aloha', with large coral-pink double flowers; 'Dortmund', single flowers, red with a white centre; 'Maigold', with beautiful semi-double, golden-yellow blooms; 'New Dawn', with the palest pink flowers; and 'Sympathie', with large, well-shaped flowers in bright scarlet. None of these is excessively tall: average height is 2.4–3 m (8–10 ft).

A SELECTION OF WALL SHRUBS
WHICH PREFER SUN

Abelia grandiflora – A medium-sized, semi-evergreen shrub with an arching habit which takes up quite a lot of space. A profusion of rather delicate pink, white and purplish flowers are produced for much of the summer. (Moderately hardy).

Acacia dealbata (mimosa) – Its evergreen, ferny foliage is joined by masses of tiny, fragrant powder-puff type yellow flowers in early spring. Unfortunately, this plant resents hard frosts and any frosts during flowering could destroy the flowers overnight. It is rather an untidy plant which needs quite a lot of space. (Not fully hardy).

Carpenteria californica – An unusual evergreen shrub with large, white, fragrant anemone-like flowers during summer. It is better to allow it to assume its natural shape rather than clip it too closely. (Moderately hardy).

Ceanothus – Mostly evergreen shrubs. Those with small, dark green leaves like *Ceanothus dentatus* are the neatest. Most have masses of rich or light blue powder-puff type flowers in spring or summer. *Ceanothus* 'Delight' is reputed to be one of the hardiest, but all resent severe winters.

Chimonanthus fragrans (winter sweet) – A deciduous shrub with strongly scented creamy yellow flowers in midwinter. The plant looks rather uninteresting for the rest of the year and does take up quite a lot of space. It seldom needs more than the occasional wall support. (Moderately hardy).

Fremontodendron californicum – Has rather striking foliage which is covered in brown hairs underneath. The shallow yellow cup-shaped flowers are produced all summer. The plant may grow quite tall and take up a lot of space generally. (Moderately hardy).

Ficus carica (fig) – Needs plenty of space but can be trained back quite neatly to a wall. The leaves are large and distinctive. Figs begin to form in early summer which, in warmer districts, ripen by late summer. The fig seems to be surprisingly hardy, though no fruits may be produced in colder districts. It is best to restrict the roots of the fig, say in a concrete "box", to curb excessive vigour.

Magnolia grandiflora – The evergreen magnolia which has large glossy mid-green leaves. It grows very tall and does not look right pruned hard back. It is, therefore, only really suitable against high walls with plenty of space. As the plant grows older, it produces large, singular creamy white flowers during summer. (Moderately hardy).

Piptanthus laburnifolius – A tall and rather untidy shrub with large trifoliate laburnum-like leaves. Upright racemes of pea-shaped yellow flowers are produced in early summer. (Moderately hardy).

Fan-trained Peaches and Nectarines – Traditional favourites for sunny walls. One of the biggest problems is the incidence of peach leaf curl – a fungus disease which can partially defoliate the plant, especially in cool, damp districts. The flowers are susceptible to frost damage.

CLIMBING AND RAMBLER ROSES

The differences between these two types of roses are so important that they are worth special mention. (Fig 20).

Climbing roses have rather gnarled stems from which flowering shoots and new branches grow. This stem system is usually regarded as permanent and is kept trained against the wall or fence and is only cut back to make room for a new stem if that should prove necessary. Climbing roses are therefore ideal on walls since, although vigorous, they can be easily controlled. Most climbing roses produce flowers (often of the large-flowered type) throughout the summer, and they are said to be recurrent flowering.

Rambler roses produce a profusion of long arching branches from the base each year, in the same fashion as a blackberry. These have to be tied back to a trellis or wires and will flower the following summer. After flowering, these branches are cut down to near the base to leave room for the next crop. Flowering usually occurs in one prolific burst and many of the flowers are borne in dense clusters of small, single or double roses. All this takes up a lot of space making the rambler rose less suitable for house walls, though ideal for trellis and many fences. Rambler roses are a particularly appropriate choice for cottage gardens.

Rambler or climbing roses and clematis can all be grown up and over

Opposite: The catkins on this *Garrya elliptica* make it a spectacular plant for a north-facing wall.

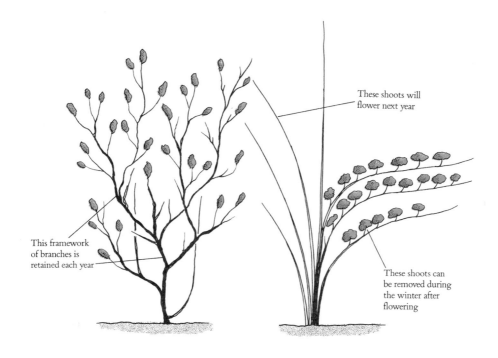

These shoots will
flower next year

This framework
of branches is
retained each year

These shoots can
be removed during
the winter after
flowering

Fig. 20 The difference in growth and pruning between (a) climbing roses, and (b) rambler roses.

old trees and shrubs, especially fruit trees, giving some welcome flowers among the otherwise uninteresting foliage. However, pruning all the plants concerned can be awkward, and the overall effect is very informal, even untidy.

CLEMATIS

These plants are worth a closer look because of their widespread popularity. There are various types of clematis. Some have large flowers like pale, purple-pink and carmine striped 'Nelly Moser' or lavender-blue 'President', both varieties of *Clematis patens*. They produce flowers on short growths emerging from the previous season's wood, so when pruning take care not to remove too much of this older growth before flowering in early summer. After flowering, the older wood can be cut back to a strong pair of buds so that new growth can be produced and ripened in time for the following year's flowering. A similar technique can be used for 'W.E. Gladstone', a *Clematis lanuginosa* variety with very large pale lavender flowers.

Clematis × *jackmanii* (violet-purple) and others like 'Barbara Jackman' and 'Gipsy Queen', along with *Clematis viticella* types like 'Ernest Markham' and 'Ville de Lyon' are pruned quite differently. In the very early spring, before growth starts, nearly all the previous year's growth is cut hard back to healthy buds. The resulting new growth produces flowers from about midsummer onwards. If high screening is needed, some of the older shoots can be kept.

Clematis montana, which produces great masses of small pink or white flowers in spring, can be pruned quite hard immediately after flowering, by which time a number of vigorous new shoots will have started to grow. A large number of these shoots can be tied in to produce next year's flowers. If left unpruned, *Clematis montana* is capable of covering whole buildings, but it can undermine house tiles and invade living space.

Clematis tangutica is unusual in producing lantern-shaped flowers late in the summer.

Clematis armandii, while not as hardy as some of the others, can be left unpruned so that maximum benefit is gained from its useful evergreen foliage. In chalky or alkaline districts, wild clematis can be seen growing strongly over hedgerows, indicating that this type of soil is probably the most suitable. But any soil seems to suit clematis, as long as it is well drained.

FRUITING SCREENS

In the garden, it might help to have a productive fruit screen but these often demand more attention than many of the other, more decorative types. The most likely climbing plants to use are the cultivated blackberry and loganberry (*Rubus*), or vines (grapes).

The blackberry or loganberry's long new trailing shoots will need tying to horizontal wires. There will usually be a mixture of older, fruiting branches, and younger rapidly growing shoots. If room permits, it could be best to keep the fruiting shoots tied to wires but let the new shoots grow freely, not tying them down until the end of summer when all the older, fruiting shoots can be cut away, freeing the wires. Apart from the new shoots later in the summer, the overall effect can be quite neat and compact but space immediately in front of the screen is needed for picking fruit and tying in.

Vines grow quite differently, as they rely on a permanent branch system. This may become quite extensive and heavy when carrying fruit, so substantial wires or fixings are essential. A sunny aspect and a sheltered fence or wall are best. (Blackberries and loganberries are less fussy).

An area of cultivated border immediately around the base of the vine will help to ensure strong growth. Vines seem to be less vigorous when grown in small borders surrounded by concrete or paving. Damp, shaded aspects may encourage mildew which can seriously disfigure the grapes. Pruning usually shortens the current season's growth back to two or three buds from the main stem in winter. One of the most popular cultivars is 'Black Hamburgh', suitable outdoors in sheltered districts or in a cold greenhouse.

ESPALIER AND CORDON FRUIT TREES

Both types are generally apples, pears or plums. Peaches and nectarines can be trained in this way but are more likely to be fan-trained (as are cherries).

THE CORDON
Cordons comprise a main stem fixed at an angle of 45°–60° on horizontal wires or some other permanent structure. Planted 90–180 cm (3–6 ft) apart, depending upon the vigour of the rootstocks involved, they produce quite a dense screen up to about 1.8 m (6 ft) high. Pruning usually involves cutting back new growth in winter to within a few buds of the main stem which encourages the production of fruiting 'bourses' — clusters of fruit/flower buds.

ESPALIERS
These have a central vertical stem with horizontal branches to left and right, fixed horizontally to wires or a wall or fence. Because of this horizontal growth, fewer plants are needed. Potentially, espaliers can be grown higher than cordons but must then have substantial support. Pruning is similar to that given to cordons once the main framework has been formed. Although growth is neat and compact, space is needed in front of the screen for training, pruning and fruit picking. Best fruiting is obtained by growing these plants against a sheltered and reasonably sunny wall or fence, avoiding early morning sun if possible.

Opposite: Clematis armandii – a valuable evergreen climber. Its creamy white flowers are an added bonus.

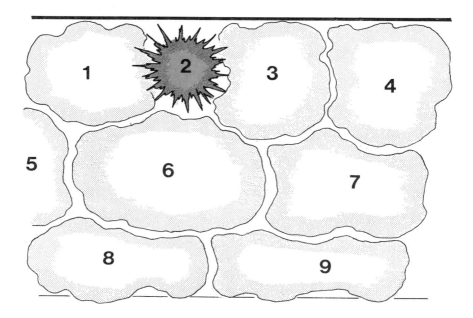

Fig. 21 A collection of shrubs which, when mature, will produce an attractive and hardy screen in almost any soil.

1. *Cotoneaster watereri.*
2. × *Cupressocyparis leylandii* 'Castlewellan' (conifer).
3. *Corylus maxima* 'Purpurea'.
4. *Philadelphus* 'Virginal'.
5. *Hippophae rhamnoides.*
6. *Berberis julianae.*
7. *Deutzia* 'Mont Rose'.
8. *Senecio laxifolius.*
9. *Potentilla arbuscula.*

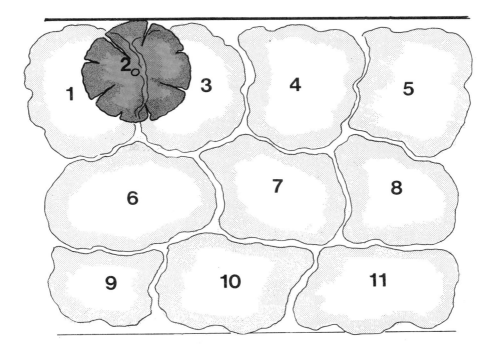

Fig. 22 A collection of mainly shrubby plants which would produce an attractive screen, preferably in acid soil.

1. *Elaeagnus pungens* 'Maculata'.
2. *Prunus × blireana* (tree).
3. Deep pink rhododendron (large).
4. *Rubus giraldianus.*
5. *Elaeagnus × ebbingei.*
6. Lacecap hydrangea (pink).
7. *Berberis × ottawensis* 'Purpurea'.
8. *Philadelphus coronarius* 'Aureus'.
9. *Caryopteris × clandonensis.*
10. *Skimmia japonica* 'Foremanii'.
11. *Hebe cupressoides.*

FAN-TRAINED PEACHES AND NECTARINES

Both need a warm sunny fence or wall. Each plant takes up a considerable amount of lateral space (like an espalier). Pruning is done in summer rather than winter and care is needed not to remove too many fruit buds, though the fan shape must be maintained so as not to clutter the plant with excessive growth.

All but perhaps one or two cultivars of blackberry are unfortunately deciduous, so they provide little screening during the winter. Growing other plants through cordons and espaliers is not really very successful and generally interferes with fruit production.

MIXED PLANT SCREENS

If there is space, mixed screens (Figs. 21 & 22) can offer the perfect combination of privacy, wind protection and an attractive, all-the-year-round appearance. When used decoratively plants are chosen very much

Fig. 23 Using trees and shrubs to produce a mixed and three-dimensional informal screen. The border would need to be quite wide.

for their usefulness in a display. In the first instance, trees are useful because they hold their often attractive foliage high on a stem. Shrubs can fill in the gap between the top of this stem and the ground and conifers produce pinnacles of evergreen foliage from the ground to almost any height. A mixed screen has to be far more three dimensional (Fig. 23).

Among the shrubs should be some evergreens, some with coloured foliage and others grown mainly for their flowers. In winter, besides the evergreens, there are shrubs with coloured stems and others that are in flower. It takes an artistic eye to create an attractive mix of colour, shape and texture. A good knowledge of how tall and wide each plant is likely to grow is also necessary to achieve the necessary screening. Care will be needed not to include acid loving plants in a chalky (alkaline) area nor half-hardy plants in a very cold district. Planting distances will depend on how large the plants are when they are put in and how many years are available for the screen to develop to an acceptable size. Eventually, of course, plants will begin to grow too large and will need careful, inconspicuous pruning or replacing with younger plants.

HONEY FUNGUS (Armillaria mellea)

Many pests and diseases affect garden plants but perhaps none is as universal as honey fungus. This feeds on and multiplies in rotting tree stumps and roots which have been left in the ground. At certain times of the year, small honey-coloured mushrooms appear close to the ground in clusters from the rotting wood. Sooner or later the branches or mycelium of the fungus travel underground, often through humus, in search of new sources of food – which could well be a living and healthy tree or shrub. Suddenly a branch or two will die, often during the summer, for no apparent reason. It may take several years for a large tree to die completely. A small portion of a hedge may die out one year, then gradually extend in both directions in subsequent years. Privet, *Ligustrum ovalifolium*, which is often used for hedging, is particularly prone to honey fungus.

Thin black strands of the fungus's mycelium, looking rather like flattened black bootlaces, can often be found under loose bark close to the ground. There will also be a strong 'mushroom' smell.

Prevention is far more reliable than any cure, so remove all old stumps and rotten branches, especially if these are parts of an infected tree or shrub. A treatment, involving the injection of a liquid into the ground *may* be successful in protecting so far unaffected plants. This is carried out by specialists as special equipment is needed.

INDEX